FUN IN TAIWAN!

The Best Guide to Taiwan

AUTHOR
Andrew Crosthwaite

PROOFREADERS
Cheryl Robbins and Zachary Fillingham

+ MP3

Fun in Taiwan!
The Best Guide to Taiwan

Cosmos Culture Ltd.
Tel: +886-(0)2-2365-9739
Fax: +886-(0)2-2365-9835
Website: www.cosmoselt.com
Email: onlineservice@icosmos.com.tw

ISBN: 978-986-318-098-2

First Published 2014

Author • Andrew Crosthwaite
Proofreader • Cheryl Robbins, Zachary Fillingham
Editor • Peggy Ting
Graphic designer • Peggy Ting

Table of Contents

Unit 2

Unit 3

Unit 4

Unit 5

Unit 6

01

Unit 1

Taiwan— The Big Picture

Taiwan might be a small country, but it is a **diverse**[1] land with a **fascinating**[2] history, beautiful scenery, **a wide range of**[3] cultures, and a strong economy. Visitors to the country might be surprised by just how much there is to see, do, and experience.

The history books generally say that Taiwan was discovered in 1544 by Portuguese sailors, but people have actually been making their way here for tens of thousands of years. As a result, there are many different cultures and ethnic groups on the island. In addition to various Chinese ethnic groups, Taiwan **is home to**[4] a large number of indigenous tribes. More recent immigration has brought people from Southeast Asia and Western nations, and they have also had an impact on everyday life in the country.

Since Taiwan is made up of so many different ethnic groups, a lot of languages are spoken here. In addition to the official language of Mandarin Chinese, there are indigenous languages, Hakka, and Taiwanese Hokkien, which is spoken by much of the population. Recent governments have also worked hard to promote English. Students have to learn the language from an early age, and it can also be seen on official signs throughout Taiwan.

Widespread[5] immigration has also affected Taiwanese religious practices. But whereas languages have generally remained separate, different religions have **blended**[6] together. The majority of people now follow a faith that is a mix of Buddhism, Taoism, and traditional folk beliefs. Owing to all of these religious influences, Taiwan is now home to hundreds of different gods that are worshipped in thousands of temples around the island. People worship these gods and their ancestors by offering incense, paper money, which is also called joss paper, and food.

Looking around Taiwan, visitors will quickly notice that there's a big difference between Taiwan's urban and rural areas. Towns and cities are usually highly developed with shops and restaurants lining the streets. On the **outskirts**[7] of built-up areas, you will find factories, industrial zones, and technology parks. Taiwan's economy has **come a long way**[8] in the last 60 to 70 years. In the early 20th century, it was dominated by agriculture, but it developed quickly after the 1950s. During the 1980s, Taiwan was one of the world's largest manufacturers and it has since developed into a center for hi-tech innovation.

Away from the bright lights and industry of the towns and cities, Taiwan's natural scenery is **breathtaking**[9]. Both local people and tourists from around the world enjoy visiting the country's holiday destinations. The Central Mountain Range offers great scenery and enjoyable hikes. Relaxation can be had at Sun Moon Lake or at one of Taiwan's many hot spring resorts, and sandy beaches dot the northern, eastern, and southern coastlines.

Taiwan might be a small place, but it makes a big impact on anyone who learns about it or decides to **pay a visit**[10].

---

1 diverse a.
2 fascinating a.
3 a wide range of
4 be home to
5 widespread a.
6 blend v.
7 outskirts n.
8 come a long way
9 breathtaking a.
10 pay a visit

Chapter 1 Landscape and Climate

Vocabulary

1 located a.
2 landscape n.
3 idyllic a.
4 boundary n.
5 as a result
6 uninhabitable a.
7 in addition to
8 species n.
9 mere a.
10 humid a.
11 urban a.
12 rural a.

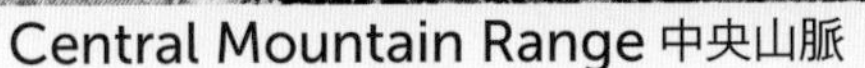

Central Mountain Range 中央山脈

Yehliu 野柳

Reading 02

Taiwan is located[1] in East Asia. To its west is the Taiwan Strait, which separates the island from China, and the Pacific Ocean lies off its east coast. With a total area of only 35,801 km^2, Taiwan is a small island. Despite its size, Taiwan is home to a variety of landscapes[2] including towering mountains, sun-kissed beaches, coral reefs, and idyllic[3] lakes. It's one of the most beautiful and geographically varied countries in the world.

The surface of the earth is made up of several massive plates of land, called tectonic plates, and Taiwan sits at the boundary[4] of two of them. Millions of years ago, these plates began pushing against one another, causing the land to rise. As a result[5], the center of Taiwan is covered by huge mountains.

Jade Mountain, or Yushan 玉山 as it's known in Chinese, is Taiwan's highest peak, measuring 3,952 meters in height. It's situated in Nantou County 南投縣 in the center of the country, and like many of the island's mountains, it's surrounded by thick forests. Hikers climbing the mountain are able to enjoy amazing views.

Taiwan's tall mountains reach all the way to the sea along lengthy sections of the east coast, and there are even mountains close to the capital city of Taipei in the north. Western Taiwan is quite different, though, as it is mostly flat. Since the country's mountainous center is mostly uninhabitable[6], many Taiwanese people live on the western plains. Much of the country's rice and wheat are grown there as well.

Sandy beaches can be found at Fulong 福隆 in the north and around Kenting 墾丁 in the south. In addition to[7] its beaches, Kenting is also famous for its coral reefs, which contain hundreds of species[8] of fish.

Taiwan is actually made up of a number of islands. On top of the main island, which is called Taiwan, there's also Green Island 綠島 and Orchid Island 蘭嶼 in the Pacific Ocean as well as a few island groups in the Taiwan Strait. The Matsu Islands 馬祖列島 lie northwest of Taiwan and are only about 20 km from the Chinese coast. Further south, Kinmen 金門 is a mere[9] 2 km from China. The Penghu Islands 澎湖群島 to the southeast of Kinmen are much closer to Taiwan.

Yushan 玉山

Kenting 墾丁

Fulong 福隆

Although the weather in Taiwan is mostly warm and humid[10], the winters can get quite cold, especially in the north. In Taipei, it's not unusual for the temperature to fall below 15°C in the winter. High up in the central mountains, it often snows between December and February. In other parts of the country, the difference between summer and winter is less obvious. In fact, Taiwan's most southerly region is called Hengchun 恆春, which means "constant spring" in Chinese.

Most of Taiwan's rain falls in the summer months, and July through September is the typhoon season. These extreme weather systems bring strong winds and heavy rain, and they can cause a lot of damage in both urban[11] and rural[12] areas.

Hehuanshan 合歡山

Hengchun 恆春

Kinmen 金門

Twin Hearts Stone Tidal Weir on the Penghu Islands
澎湖群島的雙心石滬

Dongyong Lighthouse on the Matsu Islands
馬祖列島的東湧燈塔

Reading Comprehension

Choose the correct answer based on the Reading.

________ **1. Based on the passage, which of the following geographical features does Taiwan have?** (Supporting Details)

ⓐ Volcanoes. ⓑ Very long rivers.
ⓒ Deserts. ⓓ Beautiful lakes.

________ **2. What is said about Taiwan's mountains?** (Supporting Details)

ⓐ They aren't all very tall.
ⓑ Many are surrounded by trees.
ⓒ They're mostly in the south.
ⓓ Lots of rice is grown there.

________ **3. "Kenting is also famous for its coral reefs, which contain hundreds of species of fish." "Species" is a more scientific word for ________.** (Words in Context)

ⓐ shapes ⓑ rules ⓒ movements ⓓ types

________ **4. What is the main idea of paragraph seven?** (Main Idea)

ⓐ The weather in Taiwan gets warmer the further south you go.
ⓑ In the winter there's often snow on the high mountains.
ⓒ The temperature in Taipei sometimes falls below 15°C.
ⓓ The weather in Taiwan can be very humid.

________ **5. What is implied about the weather in Hengchun?** (Making Inferences)

ⓐ The weather is very good in springtime.
ⓑ The weather is very bad in wintertime.
ⓒ The weather is very good all through the year.
ⓓ The weather changes a lot throughout the year.

Dialogs

1 gorge n.
2 valley n.
3 cliff n.
4 ferry n.
5 saltwater a.
6 fantastic a.
7 blossom n.

Taroko Gorge 太魯閣峽谷

03

Taking a trip in Taiwan

Ivy	I'm thinking about taking a trip around Taiwan. Where do you think I should go?
Tom	It depends on what kinds of things you want to see and do.
Ivy	Hmm, I suppose I'd like to go for a good hike and then go somewhere else to relax.
Tom	Well, there are lots of big mountains in Taiwan like Alishan 阿里山, Yushan, and Hehuanshan 合歡山, but my favorite place to go hiking is Taroko **Gorge**[1] 太魯閣峽谷.
Ivy	I haven't heard of it. What is it like?
Tom	It's a huge gorge in Hualien County 花蓮縣. If you go there, you'll travel through a narrow **valley**[2] with tall, rocky **cliffs**[3] rising up on either side of you.
Ivy	Sounds great. So where can I go to relax?
Tom	Why not take a **ferry**[4] from Taitung 台東 out to Green Island? It has some beaches, and there's also a rare **saltwater**[5] hot spring.
Ivy	**Fantastic**[6]! I think I know where to go on my trip. Thanks, Tom.

04

Talking about when to visit Taiwan

Steven	Hi, Lisa. After hearing you talk about Taiwan so much, I think I'd like to go there on holiday.
Lisa	Great, I think you'll love it. When are you going to go?
Steven	I don't really know. When do you think would be the best time of year?
Lisa	That's a hard question to answer. Summer is nice and hot, but it's often humid and it can rain a lot, too.
Steven	There are typhoons in the summer as well, right?
Lisa	Yeah, Taiwan usually experiences a few typhoons every year.
Steven	OK, what about winter?
Lisa	It's nice in the south during winter, but it gets quite cold in the northern areas and in the mountains.
Steven	That doesn't sound good. What about spring?
Lisa	Spring might be perfect. It's not too hot or cold, there's no chance of a typhoon, and you might even get to see the cherry **blossoms**[7] on the trees in the mountains.
Steven	You've convinced me. Spring it is!

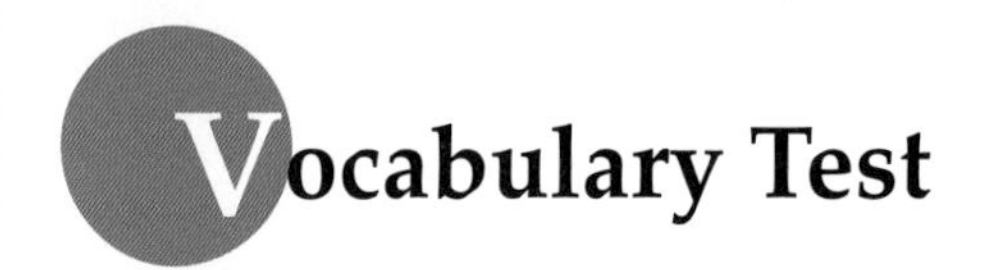

Vocabulary Test

Choose the correct word(s) to complete each sentence.

- humid
- Saltwater
- as a result
- uninhabitable
- rural
- boundary
- In addition to
- ferry
- landscapes
- cherry blossoms
- located in
- fantastic

1. Since Taiwan lies on the Tropic of Cancer, the weather is usually hot and ________ in the summer.
2. Sun Moon Lake is ________ Nantou County, which is the only landlocked county in Taiwan.
3. Towering mountains, sun-kissed beaches, and coral reefs are common ________ you can find in Taiwan.
4. Most Taiwanese people live on the western plains because the country's mountainous center is mostly ________.
5. During the typhoon season, strong winds and heavy rain cause lots of damage in both urban and ________ areas.
6. If you want to go to Green Island, you need to take a ________ from Taitung.
7. In spring, groups of tourists visit the mountains to admire the ________.
8. Taiwan sits at the ________ of Eurasian and Philippine Sea plates.
9. Taroko Gorge is a ________ place to go hiking and to enjoy incredible scenery.
10. ________ hot springs are rare, but you can find one on Green Island.
11. ________ the hot weather in summer, heavy storms are also common.
12. Western Taiwan is quite flat, and ________, it has the largest population.

More Facts About Taiwan

Alishan 阿里山

Alishan is Taiwan's most popular mountain resort area. People go there to ride the famous Alishan mountain train, and to see forests of ancient trees, cloud and mist formations, and beautiful sunsets and sunrises. When people visit Alishan, they often wake up early and ride the train to a sunrise viewing platform.

Orchid Island 蘭嶼

Orchid Island lies to the southeast of Taiwan, and it is generally much warmer than the rest of the country. The landscapes are mostly volcanic, and hard black rock can be seen throughout the island. Despite its name, Orchid Island is not covered with flowers. Instead, there are numerous paddies for growing taro root.

Shifen Waterfall 十分瀑布

As Taiwan is so mountainous, it has hundreds of waterfalls. One of the most beautiful is Shifen Waterfall, which is located in Pingxi 平溪 in northern Taiwan. Although it's only about 20 meters high, it measures 40 meters across, and many people say it looks like a mini Niagara Falls.

Monsoon Winds 季風

Temperatures in the winter can fall quickly in Taiwan because of the monsoon winds, which blow in from Central Asia. The winds are felt most strongly in the Penghu Islands, but all of the islands in the Taiwan Strait suffer relatively cold winters.

Typhoon Morakot 莫拉克颱風

In 2009, Taiwan was hit by Typhoon Morakot. It dumped close to 3,000 mm of rain on parts of Taiwan, and it was the worst typhoon the country had ever experienced. The heavy rainfall caused massive landslides, and an entire village in Kaohsiung County was buried in mud. Hundreds of people died as a result of Morakot, and total damages amounted to over NT$100 billion.

Photo by NASA

Chapter 2 Reflecting on the Past

Vocabulary

1 historian n.	6 be driven from	11 brutally adv.
2 archaeologist n.	7 set one's sights on	12 significant a.
3 indigenous a.	8 bolster v.	13 Communist n.
4 migrate v.	9 inhabitant n.	14 democratic a.
5 catch sight of	10 harsh a.	

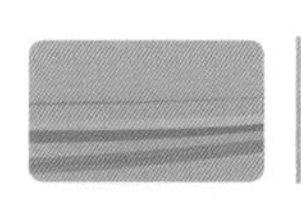

Reading  05

Many historians[1] believe that people have lived in Taiwan for at least 30,000 years, but we don't know very much about what these first peoples were like or where they came from. The only reason we know they even existed is because archaeologists[2] have found ancient skeletons and objects like bowls and tools. Another group of people came to Taiwan from Southwestern China about 6,000 to 8,000 years ago. They were the ancestors of Taiwan's present-day indigenous[3] people, and it is also thought that some of them migrated[4] to other islands. Actually, some historians believe that the indigenous peoples in countries as far away as Madagascar and New Zealand originally came from Taiwan.

The next important event in Taiwanese history came in 1544 when Portuguese sailors caught sight of[5] the island. They apparently loved Taiwan's natural scenery, because they called it "Ilha Formosa," which means "Beautiful Island." The first Westerners to actually occupy Taiwan were the Dutch in 1624.

Statue of Koxinga
國姓爺的雕像

They wanted to use the island as a base for trade with Japan. They based themselves on the western plains and established their capital in Tainan 台南. Dutch rule of Taiwan didn't last very long, however. They were driven from[6] the island in 1662 by a Chinese force led by Zheng Chenggong 鄭成功, or Koxinga 國姓爺 as he is more commonly known.

Over the next 200 years, Chinese immigrants began arriving in Taiwan in large numbers, and by the early 1800s there were more than two million people living on the island. Despite its growing population, China's emperors did not consider the territory to be important until the middle of the 19th century. That was when Japan and European nations once again began to set their sights on[7] Taiwan. The Chinese tried to bolster[8] Taiwan's coastline defenses, but they could not stop the Japanese from taking control of the island in 1895 following the first Sino-Japanese War.

Japanese control of Taiwan was marked by rapid economic and social development. They built roads and railway tracks and established banks, schools, and hospitals. Yet the Japanese are still unpopular with many of the island's inhabitants[9] as they were harsh[10] rulers who

↑ The former U.S. president Dwight D. Eisenhower visiting Taipei in a car with the former president Chiang Kai-shek in 1960

brutally[11] punished anyone who opposed them. Their occupation of Taiwan ended in 1945, when they were defeated in World War II and were forced to leave the island.

Possibly the most significant[12] development in Taiwan's recent history came in 1949. That was when the Communists[13] took control of China after a long civil war against the country's Nationalist Party, known as the Kuomintang 國民黨, or KMT. The KMT, led by Chiang Kai-shek fled to Taiwan and established its government on the island. An estimated one and a half to two million Chinese people accompanied the KMT to Taiwan.

Taiwan has changed a lot over the years, and one of the latest developments came in 1996 when the first democratic[14] presidential election was held.

A simulation of Taiwan's prehistoric life ↘

Reading Comprehension

Choose the correct answer based on the Reading.

.... **1. What is said in the passage about Taiwan's indigenous people?** (Supporting Details)

ⓐ They arrived on the island about 30,000 years ago.
ⓑ They sailed from Taiwan and settled far and wide.
ⓒ We know almost nothing about their ancestors.
ⓓ Many moved to China around 6,000 to 8,000 years ago.

.... **2. Which of the following is the correct sequence of events?** (Sequencing)

ⓐ The Dutch occupied Taiwan, then the Chinese, and then the Japanese.
ⓑ The Chinese occupied Taiwan, then the Japanese, and then the Dutch.
ⓒ The Japanese occupied Taiwan, then the Dutch, and then the Chinese.
ⓓ The Japanese occupied Taiwan, then the Chinese, and then the Dutch.

.... **3. In the third paragraph, the author mentions that "China's emperors did not consider the territory to be important." What does "territory" here refer to?** (Words in Context)

ⓐ Koxinga's army.
ⓑ Portuguese sailors.
ⓒ The island of Taiwan.
ⓓ Taiwan's indigenous people.

.... **4. The author tells Taiwan's history ....** (Clarifying Devices)

ⓐ in alphabetical order
ⓑ from the present to the past
ⓒ in random order
ⓓ from the past to the present

.... **5. What is the main idea expressed in the passage?** (Main Idea)

ⓐ The earliest record of people in Taiwan goes back 30,000 years.
ⓑ There were both good and bad aspects to Japanese rule.
ⓒ Over the centuries, Taiwan has undergone many political changes.
ⓓ Taiwan has recently entered a new era of democracy.

Overview of Fort Zeelandia (now Anping Fort), painted around 1635

Dialogs

1 sightseeing a.
2 defeat v.
3 set up
4 tax v.
5 leader n.
6 compulsory a.
7 malaria n.
8 oppose v.

06

Talking about Dutch rule in Taiwan

Cathy	I heard you're going to Tainan tomorrow.
Pete	That's right. I'm going on a sightseeing[1] trip with a friend. Where do you think we should go?
Cathy	You should definitely visit Anping Fort 安平古堡. That's where the Dutch were based when they controlled Taiwan.
Pete	The Dutch were in Taiwan?
Cathy	Yeah, you didn't know? They ruled the island for almost 40 years.
Pete	Wow! So how long ago was that?
Cathy	It all happened in the 17th century. They had to leave when a Chinese army came and defeated[2] them.
Pete	Did the Dutch do anything good for the people of Taiwan?
Cathy	They set up[3] some schools, but they also tried to tax[4] people.
Pete	Oh, OK. Were they unpopular leaders[5]?
Cathy	Some people may not have liked their rule. At Anping Fort, you'll see a statue of the man who led the army that defeated them.
Pete	What was his name?
Cathy	Koxinga 國姓爺.

07

Asking about the Japanese occupation of Taiwan

Student	Is it true that the Japanese built the Alishan railway line?
Teacher	Yes, that's correct. The Japanese built lots of railway lines around the island while they were in charge here.
Student	What else did they do here?
Teacher	They did quite a lot for business, and the economy grew during their rule. They were even responsible for establishing the Bank of Taiwan.
Student	I didn't know that.
Teacher	Yeah, they also made elementary school **compulsory**[6].
Student	Oh, that's a good thing.
Teacher	And then they built hospitals and brought doctors over from Japan because lots of people were dying from diseases like **malaria**[7].
Student	It seems like they were really good rulers.
Teacher	Um, I don't think I would ever say that. Although they did a lot of good things here, they severely punished anyone who **opposed**[8] them.
Student	Oh, right. So they were both good and bad leaders, right?
Teacher	Yes, that would be fair to say.

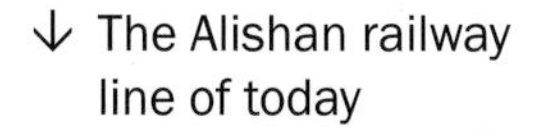
↓ The Alishan railway line of today

← National Museum of Taiwan Literature was a government building during Japanese rule.

Vocabulary Test

Match the words to the correct definitions.

____ 1. **brutally**
____ 2. **indigenous**
____ 3. **historian**
____ 4. **Communist**
____ 5. **harsh**
____ 6. **be driven from**
____ 7. **significant**
____ 8. **migrate**
____ 9. **bolster**
____ 10. **archeologist**
____ 11. **democratic**
____ 12. **inhabitant**

a original
b be forced out of
c someone who studies the past
d describing a system where everyone has a vote
e someone who lives in a particular place
f go and live in another place
g someone who thinks all workers should be rewarded equally
h to strengthen
i in a cruel way
j someone who digs up old things
k not very nice
l important

More Facts About Taiwan

Spanish Rule of Taiwan

The Dutch weren't the only European people in Taiwan in the 17th century. The Spanish arrived in 1626 and took control of parts of northern Taiwan. They built Fort San Salvador 聖薩爾瓦多城 in Keelung 基隆 and another fort in Danshui 淡水. Their stay on the island didn't last long, however. In 1642, they were attacked and defeated by a force of Dutch and indigenous troops.

Qing-Ming Divisions

Koxinga and his troops were loyal to the Ming Dynasty rulers of China. They came to Taiwan when Qing forces took control of China. In the early 1680s, around 20 years after Koxinga had died, the Qing Empire decided to wage war against his family and followers. The Imperial soldiers and navy won the military campaign and took control of Taiwan.

Eternal Golden Castle
億載金城

Built in 1875 by the Qing official Shen Baozhen（沈葆楨）

Taiwan's Wild Interior

The Qing Empire didn't achieve complete control of Taiwan. Its forces didn't travel far into the inland areas of the island for fear of upsetting the indigenous people living there. Chinese immigrants did not make their way to the east coast to develop farmland there until the late 18th century.

Learning About Taiwan's Early History

If you are interested in Taiwan's prehistoric age, one of the best places to go is the National Museum of Prehistory 國立史前文化博物館 in Taitung 台東. It was built after prehistoric remains were uncovered in Beinan Township 卑南鄉. Archeologists thought that the best way to preserve the relics would be to build a museum nearby. The National Palace Museum in Taipei also has several exhibitions of objects used by Taiwan's prehistoric peoples.

Chapter 3

Cultures, People, and Languages

Vocabulary

1	comprise v.	8	recognize v.
2	ethnic a.	9	overwhelming a.
3	as such	10	fluent a.
4	distinct a.	11	accent n.
5	categorize v.	12	exclusively adv.
6	descend v.	13	colonial a.
7	derive v.	14	open-minded a.

Reading

08

Taiwan's population of 23 million people comprises[1] a wide variety of ethnic[2] groups. As such[3], it's home to numerous languages and cultures. In some cases, the differences between them may not appear very obvious. In other cases, however, the cultural and language-related differences between two groups make them totally distinct[4] from one another.

About 70% of the population is categorized[5] as Hoklo, making them the largest ethnic group by far. The Hoklo are descended[6] from people who made their way to Taiwan from China's Fujian Province 福建省 in the 17th and 18th centuries.

There is another group of Chinese people that migrated to Taiwan. They are called the Hakka, and their name derives[7] from the Chinese for "traveler" or

The Bunun（布農族） is one of Taiwan's indigenous tribes.

Fried Pig's intestines with Ginger（薑絲炒大腸） is a famous Hakka food.

Taiwanese children learn to speak English at young age.

"guest." It is thought that they might have moved southward from different regions of China before making their way to Taiwan. Due to Qing era restrictions on travel to Taiwan from certain areas of China, such as Guangdong Province 廣東省 where many Hakka lived, the Hakka arrived in Taiwan later than the Hoklo. Today, the Hakka make up about 14% of Taiwan's population.

There is also the people who came to Taiwan with Chiang Kai-shek in the late 1940s and early 1950s. This group, along with their children, are sometimes referred to as Mainlanders.

Taiwan also has a large number of indigenous people. Officially, only 2% of the population belongs to this group. The government recognizes[8] 14 different indigenous Taiwanese tribes, each of which has its own culture and language.

In addition to these groups, Taiwan is home to a considerable number of foreign residents. In early 2011, Taiwan's National Immigration Agency reported that there were over 430,000 foreigners living here. The overwhelming[9] majority of them, about 88%, are from Indonesia, Vietnam, the Philippines, and Thailand. There are also a large number of Westerners. Regardless of where they are from, most foreigners in Taiwan have come seeking employment opportunities.

The national language of Taiwan is Mandarin Chinese and almost everyone here is fluent[10] in it. Although it's technically the same as the

Traditional Chinese characters

official language of China, the Taiwanese speak it with a different accent[11]. Taiwan also uses a more complicated, traditional writing form, while China switched to a simplified system of writing characters in the 1950s.

Most people also speak at least some Taiwanese. This language was brought to the island by the Hoklo people, and it is sometimes referred to as Taiwanese Hokkien. Many people, especially in the south, are fluent in Taiwanese and use it instead of Mandarin in their day-to-day lives.

Hakka is also spoken in Taiwan, but almost exclusively[12] by people from that ethnic group. You might hear some older people speak in Japanese, as this language was used in schools during the Japanese colonial[13] period. And as in many other places around the world, English is becoming an important secondary language in Taiwan. Children are taught English in schools and many official signs are written in both English and Chinese.

In modern Taiwan, most people speak at least two languages. And because they have so many different cultural influences, the Taiwanese are usually quite open-minded[14] about things they're unfamiliar with.

Reading Comprehension

Choose the correct answer based on the Reading.

______ **1. "About 70% of the population is categorized as Hoklo." Another word for "categorized" is ______.** (Synonyms)

ⓐ created ⓑ grouped
ⓒ edited ⓓ praised

______ **2. What can you infer from the passage about the Hakka people?** (Making Inferences)

ⓐ Most of them left Taiwan soon after arriving.
ⓑ Most Hakka people intermarried with Taiwan's indigenous people.
ⓒ They originally came from Fujian Province.
ⓓ They arrived in Taiwan after the Hoklo.

______ **3. What is the main idea expressed in the passage?** (Main Idea)

ⓐ Taiwan is a country rich in languages and cultures.
ⓑ English is becoming more and more popular in Taiwan.
ⓒ The Hoklo people make up the majority of Taiwan's population.
ⓓ Taiwan is home to four major cultural groups.

______ **4. Where are most of Taiwan's foreign residents from?** (Supporting Details)

ⓐ Europe. ⓑ America.
ⓒ Asia. ⓓ Africa.

______ **5. What does the author say about Taiwanese people?** (Supporting Details)

ⓐ They're generally not well educated.
ⓑ They're unpleasant to foreigners.
ⓒ They're closed off from the world.
ⓓ They're receptive to new things.

Dialogs

1 diversity n.
2 racial a.
3 split v.
4 root n.
5 tribal a.

Rice cooked in bamboo（竹筒飯）—commonly eaten by Taiwan's indigenous people

09

Chatting about cultural **diversity**[1]

Sheryl	You know, I've noticed something about people in Taiwan. There doesn't seem to be a lot of diversity.
Gary	What do you mean?
Sheryl	Well, everyone's Chinese. OK, I know there are indigenous people in certain parts of Taiwan, but apart from that, there's only one ethnic group.
Gary	That's only partly true, Sheryl. There's actually quite a lot of **racial**[2] diversity.
Sheryl	Seriously? You're going to have to explain this to me.
Gary	I'd be happy to. The people you call Chinese can actually be **split**[3] up into three different groups. There are the Hoklo people who first came to Taiwan from China's Fujian Province in the 17th and 18th centuries. Then there are the Hakka who have their **roots**[4] in a different part of China. Finally, there are the Mainlanders who came here when the KMT lost the Chinese Civil War in the middle of the last century.
Sheryl	OK. I guess there's a bit more diversity than I once thought.

10

Chatting about language

Matthew	I heard that you speak a bit of Spanish.
Denise	Yeah, that's right. I used to live in southern California, and there are a lot of Spanish-speaking people from Latin America there.
Matthew	That's cool. Do you think you could teach me?
Denise	I guess so, and maybe you can teach me Chinese.
Matthew	That sounds good.
Denise	How many languages can you speak?
Matthew	Good question. I suppose my English is OK, then there's Mandarin, obviously. I also speak Amis, the language of my indigenous tribe.
Denise	Wow! Do all indigenous people speak their **tribal**[5] languages?
Matthew	No. Quite a few of my Amis friends don't speak the language, but I think it's important to keep the culture alive.
Denise	How about Taiwanese, do you speak that as well?
Matthew	I know a little, but I'm not very good at it.
Denise	That's incredible. You already speak four languages and you want to learn another.
Matthew	Ha ha. I guess I just love talking.

The Harvest Festival of the Amis

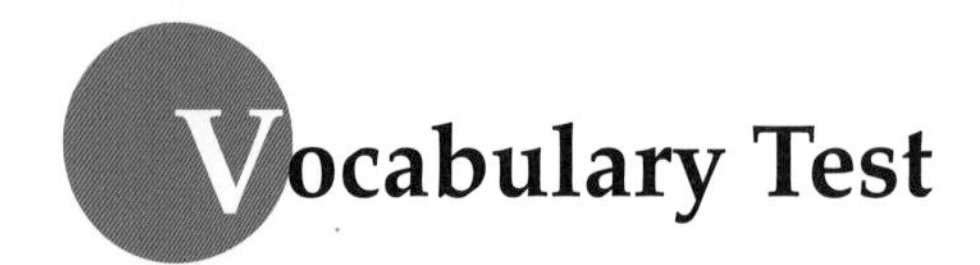

Vocabulary Test

Choose the correct word to complete each sentence.

- colonial
- racial
- comprises
- descended
- distinct
- open-minded
- fluent
- overwhelming
- categorized
- tribal

1. Many indigenous people are proud of their ____________ cultures.
2. In Taiwan, there is actually a lot of ____________ diversity; there is not only one ethnic group.
3. Most Taiwanese people are ____________ in Mandarin Chinese.
4. People from different ethnic groups may look much alike, but their cultures are still ____________ from one another.
5. Many Taiwanese people feel an ____________ desire to learn English.
6. The people who came to Taiwan with Chiang Kai-shek in the late 1940s are often ____________ as Mainlanders in this country.
7. It is said that most of Taiwan's Hakka population is ____________ from people who came from Guangdong region.
8. During the Japanese ____________ period, the Japanese language used to be taught in schools.
9. Taiwanese people have been exposed to many different cultures, so they're quite ____________.
10. The Taiwanese population ____________ many different ethnic groups including the Hakka, Hoklo, and indigenous people.

More Facts About Taiwan

Unofficial indigenous tribes

In addition to Taiwan's 14 officially recognized indigenous tribes, there are also a large number of tribes that haven't been recognized by the government. Many of these tribes have few remaining members, and in some cases, their language has completely died out. Some of these tribes, like the Pazeh 巴則海族, are actively trying to save their language and have campaigned for official recognition.

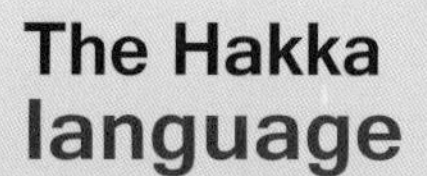

The Hakka language

The Hakka people spread far and wide throughout China and to various countries in Southeast Asia. They all speak the same basic language, but there are regional differences in pronunciation. Taiwanese Hakka has been widely influenced by Taiwanese Hokkien, but it is still possible for Hakka people from China to understand the language.

Recent immigration

Since the late 1980s, hundreds of thousands of foreign nationals have entered Taiwanese society through marriage. The majority of these marriages involve Taiwanese men and women from China or Southeast Asian countries. There are also a growing number of marriages between Taiwanese people and Westerners. This new immigration is already having an impact on culture in Taiwan, with foreign languages and foods becoming more common.

Pinyin

Pinyin is the system by which Chinese is written using the Roman alphabet—often called English letters. In Taiwan, many road and street signs are written in both Chinese and pinyin. The only problem is that many different versions of pinyin have been used in Taiwan. This means that a town or street name might be spelt differently on different signs. *Xinyi* 信義, for example, could also be written as *Hsinyi* or *Shinyi*.

Chapter 4

Religious Practice

Vocabulary

1 Buddhism n.
2 Taoism n.
3 worship v.
4 favorable a.
5 mercy n.
6 harmony n.
7 fortune n.
8 bear v.
9 regard v.
10 morality n.
11 incense n.
12 predict v.
13 missionary n.
14 Roman Catholic Church
15 estimate v.

Reading 11

As you make your way around Taiwan, one of the first things you'll notice is the temples. There are thousands of them. Some are exclusively Buddhist, but most Taiwanese temples combine Buddhism[1], Taoism[2], and traditional folk religion. In fact, you can sometimes find people worshipping[3] Buddhist and Taoist gods in the same building. The majority of people in Taiwan follow a combination of Buddhism, Taoism, and folk religion.

According to Buddhism, people are reborn when they die. If they have lived a good life, they will be born into a favorable[4] situation, but if they have lived an immoral life, they will return to an unsatisfactory position. Guanyin 觀音, the goddess of mercy[5], is an important figure in Buddhism, and her statues can be found all over Taiwan.

Taoism teaches that we should try to live in harmony[6] with the Tao, which is the true nature of the universe. Many Taoist gods are people who did great things while they were alive. One of the most famous is Guangong 關公, a Chinese general who died in 219 AD. He is now worshipped as the god of war.

↖ Guanyin

Taiwanese folk religion involves ancestor worship, fortune[7] telling, and a belief in ghosts and spirits. Mazu 媽祖, the goddess of the sea, is the most important figure in Taiwanese folk religion. Statues of her and temples bearing[8] her name can be found in many towns and cities, especially those along the coast.

To make religion in Taiwan even more interesting, there are also a large number of Confucius temples. Confucius is not really regarded[9] as a god, but his teachings on morality[10] and duty have influenced Chinese culture and religions.

Worship in Taiwan generally involves paying your respects and making offerings. In temples, people light incense[11], offer food and drink, and burn paper money for the gods. It is believed that this money is transported up to the gods when it is burnt. People also use incense and paper money to honor their ancestors. On some occasions, offerings are made to keep ghosts away.

For many Taiwanese people, visiting fortune tellers is an important practice. Many different methods are used to predict[12] a person's future, but most fortune tellers in Taiwan work by looking at a person's date and time of birth. While some people will only visit fortune tellers once or twice in their lives, others will consult them before making any important decision. Businesspeople

People worshipping ↑

Guangong 關公 →

↑ Xingtien Temple 行天宮

ask about good days to open a new company, lovers ask if their partner is a good match for them, and parents ask for advice on naming their children. It's believed that getting one of these decisions wrong could put you out of harmony with the universe, which would bring bad luck.

Taiwan also has a large Christian population. The religion was first brought to the country by Dutch missionaries[13] in the 17th century. Spanish priests from the Roman Catholic Church[14] followed, and missionaries have been making their way here ever since. It is estimated[15] that there are over a million Christians now living in Taiwan.

Reading Comprehension

Choose the correct answer based on the Reading.

.... **1. What is implied in the passage about Buddhism?** (Making Inferences)

ⓐ It teaches that our futures have already been decided.
ⓑ It teaches that we are rewarded for our good actions.
ⓒ It teaches that we are frequently visited by spirits.
ⓓ It teaches that you'll be worshipped if you're good.

.... **2. What is the third paragraph about?** (Subject Matter)

ⓐ Taoism. ⓑ Buddhism.
ⓒ Fortune telling. ⓓ Temples in Taiwan.

.... **3. Which of the following is listed as being part of Taiwanese folk religions?** (Supporting Details)

ⓐ The worship of ghosts.
ⓑ The worship of nature.
ⓒ The worship of your own spirit.
ⓓ The worship of ancestors.

.... **4. In paragraph four the author mentions that many temples bear Mazu's name. Which of the following sentences uses "bear" in the same sense as the passage does?** (Words in Context)

ⓐ He could not bear to see his daughter suffer.
ⓑ Cats can bear up to nine kittens with each pregnancy.
ⓒ The Eiffel Tower bears the name of its designer, Gustave Eiffel.
ⓓ The walls are too weak to bear the weight of the ceiling.

.... **5. Who brought Christianity to Taiwan?** (Supporting Details)

ⓐ Europeans. ⓑ Americans.
ⓒ The Chinese. ⓓ The Japanese.

Dialogs

1 honest a.
2 Jew n.
3 consult v.

12

Talking about religion

Daisy	Do you often go to the temple?
Brad	Yes, I usually go with my family about once every two weeks.
Daisy	So what kind of temple is it? Is it Buddhist or Taoist?
Brad	I don't really know to be **honest**[1] with you.
Daisy	What? How can you not know? You say you go there quite often.
Brad	Buddhism and Taoism have really gotten mixed together in Taiwan, so it's sometimes difficult to know which is which.
Daisy	Really? That seems so strange.
Brad	Strange or not, that's how it is here. A lot of people follow both religions at the same time, and a lot of temples cover both religions.
Daisy	Wow!
Brad	So this kind of thing doesn't happen in Europe?
Daisy	No. Over there, a Christian is a Christian and a **Jew**[2] is a Jew. The two religions stay separate from one another.
Brad	Hmm. It's so different to here.

The Buddha Memorial Center
佛陀紀念館

13

Talking about going to a fortune teller

Lilly	I'm going to see a fortune teller this afternoon. Do you want to come with me?
Paul	Yeah, sure. Maybe I'll get my fortune read, too.
Lilly	When was the last time you visited a fortune teller?
Paul	I don't know. My parents took me to see one when I was a kid, but that must have been about 15 years ago.
Lilly	Wow! Today will be my second trip this year.
Paul	Oh right. Do you **consult**[3] him before making any big decision?
Lilly	Yes, I do. I've just been offered a new job, so I want to know if it would be good for me to take it.
Paul	OK. What else did you see him about this year?
Lilly	I asked him about that guy I met called Brad. Do you remember him?
Paul	Yes, but I haven't seen him for a long time.
Lilly	That's because I was told we would argue a lot, so we decided to end the relationship.

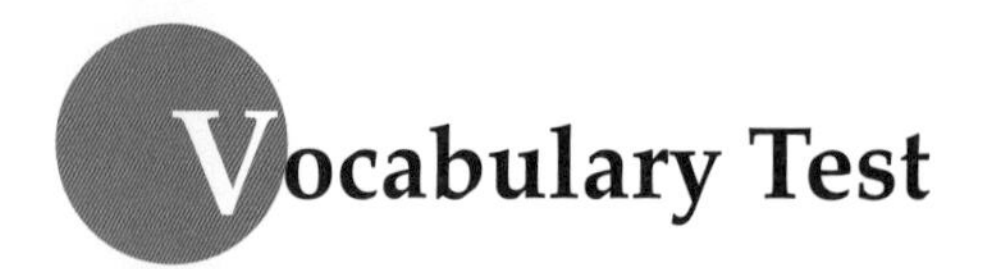

Vocabulary Test

Choose the correct word to complete each sentence.

regarded
bearing
predict
missionaries
worshipped
mercy
Buddhism
harmony
morality
incense

1. Guangong is one of the most important gods ______________ in Taiwan.
2. Guanyin, the goddess of ______________, is highly respected throughout the nation and you can find her statues all over Taiwan.
3. More and more people are learning how to live in ______________ with nature.
4. It's very common to see people lighting ______________ sticks and burning paper money in temples.
5. You can find many temples in Taiwan ______________ Mazu's name, especially along the coast.
6. Even though Confucius is not really ______________ as a god, there are still a large number of Confucius temples in Taiwan.
7. Fortune tellers use Tarot cards, astrology, and people's time and date of birth to ______________ someone's future.
8. Confucius's teachings on ______________ and duty have influenced Chinese culture and religions.
9. Christianity was first brought to Taiwan by Dutch ______________ in the 17th century.
10. ______________ is a very old religion that began in India over 2,000 years ago.

Red bedroom lights

In Taiwan, if you look at the windows of apartment blocks at nighttime, you'll notice that some have a red light coming from them. This is because some families keep a shrine in their homes to honor the gods or their ancestors. Red lamps are kept on in these shrines because red is a lucky color and it helps to keep away evil spirits.

Incense

Burning incense is an important part of worship in Taiwan, and the busier temples are usually filled with thick smoke. One reason for this is that the smoke is believed to spiritually cleanse the surrounding area. Sticks of incense are also used to help people pay their respects to the gods. In most of Taiwan's temples, people offer one stick of incense to each god or goddess worshipped in that temple.

Mormons

Taiwan has received many foreign missionaries over the years. They have come from many different countries and have introduced many different teachings. The biggest group of missionaries in Taiwan at present is from the Church of Jesus Christ of Latter Day Saints, often called the Mormon Church, which was founded in America in 1830.

Mazu has been described as "Taiwan's guardian goddess," and she is certainly one of Taiwan's most popular religious figures. Mazu was actually a real person, a girl who was born in Fujian Province in about 960 AD. Stories about her say she would wear red clothes and stand on the shore to help fishermen find their way. Another says that she saved her father when he was caught up in a storm.

Mazu

Chapter 5 Economic Development

Vocabulary

1 economic a.
2 inflation n.
3 beneficial a.
4 currency n.
5 stabilize v.
6 reform n.
7 boost n.
8 construction n.
9 nuclear a.
10 capability n.
11 semiconductor n.
12 crisis n.
13 adaptability n.
14 enterprise n.
15 trading a.

Reading 14

Taiwan is a small country in terms of both size and population, but it is still an economic[1] success story. It is ranked as one of the largest economies in the world, and people generally enjoy a high standard of living. It hasn't always been so wealthy, though. Following the Second World War, Taiwan was poor, and it was struggling with massive levels of inflation[2]. Fortunately, change came quickly in the following years. Taiwan received an injection of foreign cash and a new government introduced a series of beneficial[3] economic policies.

New Taiwanese Dollars

Farmers began to own their land and worked harder in the 1950s.

From 1950 to the late 1980s, Taiwan's economy grew so quickly that the period has been called the "Taiwan Miracle." In the thirty years between 1950 and 1980, the economy expanded by an average of almost 9% each year.

Taiwan's economic miracle really began in 1949 with the creation of the New Taiwanese Dollar. The new currency[4] helped to stabilize[5] Taiwan's finances and bring inflation under control. Then, a land reform[6] plan was introduced. Farmland was taken from large landowners and distributed to small farmers. Because these farmers now owned the land they worked on, they worked harder and produced more food. They became richer and were able to spend more money. In turn, this gave a boost[7] to Taiwan's new manufacturing industry.

Taiwan was also helped by U.S. financial aid. It's estimated that the U.S. gave as much as US$4 billion between 1945 and 1965, and that money definitely helped to speed up economic expansion.

To make sure that Taiwan could continue its success, the government implemented the "Ten Major Construction[8] Projects" in the 1970s. Among these projects were the creation of a highway from Keelung City 基隆市 to Kaohsiung City, the development of the local steel and oil industries, and the building of a nuclear[9] power plant. The completion of these works has greatly improved Taiwan's transport, manufacturing, and power capabilities[10].

From the 1980s onwards, the Taiwanese government has tried to promote high-tech industries. Science and technology parks have been built around the island and Taiwan has become a global center for flat screen technology and advanced semiconductors[11] that are used in many modern electronics.

Although economic growth has slowed since the late 1980s, Taiwan has demonstrated an ability to protect itself from regional and global economic troubles. Taiwan was not badly affected by the Asian financial

National Highway

Kaohsiung Harbor

crisis[12] in the late 1990s and it recovered quickly from the 2008 global economic crisis. It is thought that this strength comes from careful economic planning, adaptability[13] thanks to Taiwan's numerous small and medium-sized enterprises[14], and the hard work of the Taiwanese people.

Looking forward, the economy appears to be strong. Taiwan is one of the world's top trading[15] nations, and it has good connections with the rest of the world.

Reading Comprehension

Choose the correct answer based on the Reading.

.... **1. What is the main idea of the passage?** (Main Idea)

ⓐ Taiwan has developed over the years into an economic success story.

ⓑ Taiwan has good economic connections with the rest of the world.

ⓒ The people of Taiwan are known for being hard working.

ⓓ In the late 40s, Taiwan was in a bad way economically.

.... **2. According to the passage, what event marked the start of Taiwan's economic growth?** (Supporting Details)

ⓐ The end of World War Two.
ⓑ The KMT arriving in Taiwan.
ⓒ The creation of a new currency.
ⓓ A new land reform plan.

.... **3. What is implied in the passage about small farmers?** (Making Inferences)

ⓐ They wouldn't work at all for large landowners.

ⓑ They worked harder in the 1950s than in the 1940s.

ⓒ They quickly moved to the manufacturing sector.

ⓓ They were behind Taiwan's land reform laws.

.... **4. According to the passage, what effect did the 2008 economic crisis have on Taiwan?** (Supporting Details)

ⓐ It had no noticeable effect on Taiwan.

ⓑ It affected Taiwan for a short time.

ⓒ It completely devastated Taiwan.

ⓓ It affected Taiwan for a long time.

.... **5. In paragraph three, the author mentions "In turn, this gave a boost to Taiwan's new manufacturing industry." What does "this" refer to?** (Words in Context)

ⓐ Taiwan's farmers working harder.

ⓑ Taiwan's farmers owning their own land.

ⓒ The creation of the New Taiwan Dollar.

ⓓ Taiwan's farmers spending more money.

Dialogs

1 make up
2 smartphone n.
3 unemployment n.
4 shame n.

15

Talking about Taiwan's biggest industries

Jim	How was your train ride from Tainan 台南?
Nancy	It was really interesting. There's a huge amount of farmland here. It must be a huge industry in Taiwan.
Jim	Not really. I know there are a lot of rice fields, but I'm pretty sure that farming makes up[1] less than 3% of the economy.
Nancy	That's really surprising. So what are the biggest industries here?
Jim	High-tech manufacturing is quite important.
Nancy	What kinds of things are made here?
Jim	Smartphones[2], computers, flat-screen TVs, and probably a lot of other things as well.
Nancy	That's impressive. What other industries are important?
Jim	Service industries easily make up the biggest part of Taiwan's economy.
Nancy	What do you mean by the service industry?
Jim	One part of it is banking and sales, and then there are also the shops, restaurants, and places offering entertainment.
Nancy	Ha ha. That makes sense. I've noticed that people here love to eat and shop.

Night Market

Taipei 101
one of the most important business building and shopping centers in Taiwan

16

Talking about **unemployment**[3] in Taiwan

Tina	I'm really worried about my sister. She doesn't have a job. She hasn't had one for about two months.
Dave	That's a shame[4]. I was out of work a couple of years ago, and it made me very unhappy.
Tina	I think it's a big problem now in Taiwan.
Dave	What do you mean?
Tina	I'm talking about unemployment. The number of people without a job is so high at the moment.
Dave	The last I heard, the unemployment rate was about 5%.
Tina	That's right. The government should do something about it.
Dave	I think they're probably trying. You should remember that things are actually a lot worse in many other countries.
Tina	Seriously?
Dave	Yeah. In the UK the unemployment rate was almost 8% in mid-2011, and in America it was about 9%. I heard that it's about 20% in Spain.
Tina	That's terrible. I guess I should feel lucky that I'm in Taiwan.
Dave	You really should.

Vocabulary Test

Match the words to the correct definitions.

.... 1.	**stabilize**	.... 7.	**inflation**
.... 2.	**in turn**	.... 8.	**nuclear**
.... 3.	**capability**	.... 9.	**trading**
.... 4.	**economic**	.... 10.	**reform**
.... 5.	**currency**	.... 11.	**construction**
.... 6.	**adaptability**	.... 12.	**beneficial**

a. a change designed to bring improvement
b. the way a structure is built
c. relating to money and business
d. make steadier
e. describing the joining or splitting of atoms
f. an increase in prices
g. helpful
h. following on
i. a system of money
j. the ability to do something
k. buying and selling
l. the ability to change

The Japanese Colonial Era

When the Japanese ruled Taiwan, they did a number of things to get the country working better. Improving Taiwan's economy meant that they could make more money for themselves. They set up new transport and communication networks, and they also improved the local education system. These things had a huge impact on Taiwan's economy long after the Japanese had left the island.

Made in Taiwan

In the 1980s, Taiwan became famous around the world for producing cheap electronic goods and toys. Because the Made in Taiwan logo was printed on so many different products, it was seen by people everywhere. Even though Taiwan no longer manufactures so many items, people in the West still remember "Made in Taiwan."

World Leaders

Instead of making cheap goods, Taiwan now produces advanced, expensive electronics goods. Some Taiwanese companies have even become some of the biggest in the world. Apple may be the leading smartphone company, but HTC, which is based in Taoyuan 桃園, now has an international reputation for excellence. In computing, Acer and Asus are two of the world's biggest manufacturers.

The Acer headquarter in Taiwan

Biotechnology

Biotechnology is a new industry that uses tiny living creatures to develop new technologies and medicines. The Taiwanese government wants to use the country's existing knowledge in hi-tech industries to become a world leader in biotechnology. In addition to its technological skills, Taiwan has very good research facilities and adventurous businesspeople.

Unit 2

Travel and Accommodation

17

Taiwan may be a small country, but since the central regions are covered by towering mountain ranges, it isn't always the easiest place to get around.

An extensive network of roads and railways connects towns and cities along Taiwan's highly-developed west coast, providing some travel **alternatives**[1]. In addition to a regular train service, there's a high-speed rail link. Train tickets are **relatively**[2] cheap, and services are almost always clean and **punctual**[3]. **Motorists**[4] have the option of ordinary roads, broader highways, and high-speed freeways.

Traveling down the east coast isn't quite as easy, as there are no freeways or high-speed trains. Despite that, journeys between Taitung and Hualien or Yilan are **far from**[5] difficult. The problems start when you want to travel from east to west. There are roads running across the country, but they can be difficult to cross. For journeys like this, flying might be a better option.

Trips around Taiwan are made far less stressful due to the fact that a range of accommodation can be found practically everywhere in the country. Taiwan's growing number of tourists and people on business trips mean that the local hotel industry is **thriving**[6]. City accommodation ranges from the luxurious to the cheap and simple. In rural areas, resort hotels provide comfort and relaxation, while hostels provide people on tighter **budgets**[7] with a good place to stay.

If you want to really get away from **civilization**[8], you can always get a tent and head up into the mountains. There are lots of campsites in the Taiwanese countryside, and many have good **facilities**[9].

If you decide to travel around the country by car or bike, you might want to check into a motel. They're very popular here and can usually be found outside urban areas and on the edges of towns and cities. Some are simple and provide budget accommodation, but others are very comfortable and well decorated.

Urban transport is far less expensive in Taiwan than it is in the West. Taxis, even in the capital city of Taipei, are **comparatively**[10] cheap. In smaller towns, they can be the best way to get around. Bus networks run through the cities. They can be very convenient, but taking them is sometimes troublesome. Wherever you are in the world, finding out which bus you need to take is not easy, and Taiwan is no **exception**[11]. Even when you're on the right vehicle, it's hard to work out when you should stop the bus. But bus drivers here are **by and large**[12] helpful, and if you tell them where you want to go, they will tell you when to get off.

Taipei and Kaohsiung also have excellent MRT networks—that are similar to New York's subway or London's Underground. Fares are surprisingly cheap and the trains and stations are very clean. The MRT is easy to use and more stations are being built to make the systems even better.

1 **alternative** n.
2 **relatively** adv.
3 **punctual** a.
4 **motorist** n.
5 **far from**
6 **thriving** a.
7 **budget** n.
8 **civilization** n.
9 **facility** n.
10 **comparatively** adv.
11 **exception** n.
12 **by and large**

Chapter 6 Long-Distance Travel

Taiwan railway

Vocabulary

1. ferry n.
2. outlying a.
3. wind v.
4. scenic a.
5. on time
6. slash v.
7. out of reach
8. lack of
9. notoriously adv.
10. choppy a.
11. rental n.
12. troublesome a.

Reading

18

Traveling from city to city in Taiwan is very easy as you can choose from a wide variety of transportation methods. In addition to making use of bus and train services, travelers can rent cars, take airplanes, or board ferries[1] to the outlying[2] islands.

Rail lines run in a loop around Taiwan and connect the cities and almost all of the major towns. The longest line is the Western Line 西部幹線 which runs from Keelung 基隆 in the north all the way down to Kaohsiung in the south. Many of the lines, including the South Link Line 南迴線 and the Huatung Line 花東線, take passengers along routes that offer beautiful views of Taiwan's mountains and coastline. There are also a few smaller, branch lines that wind[3] their way inland along scenic[4] routes. There is regular service between popular destinations, and the trains almost always run on time[5]. In addition to the regular rail network, a high-speed rail line was established between Taipei and Kaohsiung in 2007. The 300 kmh trains run down the western side of the country, slashing[6] travel times between Taiwan's biggest cities.

Although rail tickets are not expensive, traveling by bus is usually a lot cheaper. Depending on which company you travel with, journeys can be very comfortable. Some buses are fitted with large, soft seats that seem more like armchairs than ordinary bus seats. While service doesn't run as frequently in the south or on the east coast, buses transport thousands of people around Taiwan every day in other parts of the country.

↓ Taiwan high speed rail ticket

Taiwan high speed rail

For faster travel times, you can also choose to fly. There are 18 passenger airports around Taiwan, which makes flying from one region to another extremely convenient. By taking a plane, you can cut travel times from hours to just minutes. It might seem strange for a country as small as Taiwan to have so many airports, but it seems that some people here just don't want to wait. The result is that flying between cities is easy and fairly inexpensive. Eight of Taiwan's airports are located on the outlying islands, so no part of the country is out of reach[7].

Taking ferries is an alternative way to travel around Taiwan.

Another way to travel to these smaller islands is by taking a ferry. Boat services are available from some of Taiwan's port cities, and tickets are cheaper than the average air fare. The only problem with traveling by ferry is the lack of[8] comfort. The waters surrounding Taiwan are notoriously[9] choppy[10] and ferries often rock from side to side. The journey can be a bit of a nightmare for someone who suffers from seasickness, so in the end it might be worth it to spend a little extra money on a plane ticket.

If you want more freedom over how you travel, a car rental[11] might be the best option. Rental companies can be found outside most major railway stations, and there are often discounts for people wanting to rent for more than just a couple of days.

However you choose to travel, getting around Taiwan is rarely troublesome[12].

Bus services are widely available.

Reading Comprehension

Choose the correct answer based on the Reading.

.... 1. **What is the main idea expressed in the passage?** (Main Idea)

ⓐ All of Taiwan's major cities are connected by the round-island rail line.
ⓑ By flying from place to place you can really shorten your travel times.
ⓒ With so many transport options, travel in Taiwan is very convenient.
ⓓ Ferries connect the main island of Taiwan with the smaller outlying islands.

.... 2. **According to the passage, why might people choose to travel by bus?** (Supporting Details)

ⓐ Buses are always very comfortable.
ⓑ Tickets generally cost less.
ⓒ Buses always have faster travel times.
ⓓ It's more environmentally friendly.

.... 3. **What does the author suggest about air travel in Taiwan?** (Making Inferences)

ⓐ It's surprisingly well developed.
ⓑ It is the most advanced in the world.
ⓒ It needs technological updates.
ⓓ It's the most popular transport form.

.... 4. **"The waters surrounding Taiwan are notoriously choppy and ferries often rock from side to side." If something is "choppy," it is NOT ....** (Antonyms)

ⓐ uneven ⓑ calm ⓒ rough ⓓ wild

.... 5. **According to the passage, what problem might ferry passengers encounter?** (Supporting Details)

ⓐ Expensive tickets. ⓑ Old, broken-down boats.
ⓒ Infrequent service. ⓓ Rough seas.

Dialogs

1 administration n.
2 switch v.
3 timetable n.
4 freeway n.

 19

Calling the Taiwan Railways **Administration**[1] helpline for information about a train journey

Worker	Hello, this is the Taiwan Railways Administration helpline. How can I help you?
Passenger	Hi. I'd like some information on getting from Tainan 台南 to Jiji 集集.
Worker	OK, well Jiji isn't on the main rail line. It's connected to the main network by the Jiji Branch Line.
Passenger	Does that mean I'll have to change trains somewhere?
Worker	That's correct. What you'll have to do is take a train from Tainan to Ershui 二水, and then **switch**[2] to the Jiji Line.
Passenger	That doesn't sound too difficult. How long does the trip from Ershui to Jiji take?
Worker	It should take about 40 minutes, but the line does run through some very nice countryside so it's an interesting journey.
Passenger	That sounds nice.
Worker	You should check the **timetable**[3], however, because trains along this line are not as regular as they are along the main network.
Passenger	OK, I'll do that. Thanks for the help.

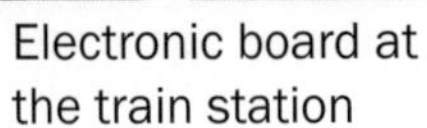
Electronic board at the train station

Train platform

Coastal highway

20

Asking for advice about getting from Taipei to Tainan

Lindsey	Hi, Paul. Have you done very much traveling around Taiwan?
Paul	A bit, yes. Why, what's wrong?
Lindsey	I've got to go down to Tainan on Monday to meet a client, and I'm not sure about the best way to get there.
Paul	You could always rent a car and drive down there.
Lindsey	I don't think so. I'm a bit scared of driving on the freeways[4] here.
Paul	There are buses, but I've always found that they're either too warm or too cold. So, I guess I'd advise taking the train.
Lindsey	OK. Does the high speed train stop in Tainan?
Paul	Yeah, well, the station's actually a little bit outside the city center, but you can easily get into the center by train, bus, or taxi.
Lindsey	That sounds good. How long will the journey take?
Paul	I'm not sure, but I'd guess about 80 minutes.

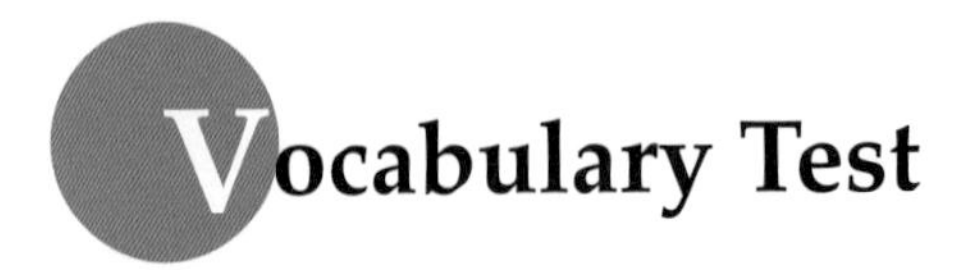

Vocabulary Test

Match the words with the correct definitions.

.... 1. **rental**	a. a terrible experience
.... 2. **on time**	b. beautiful
.... 3. **outlying**	c. according to schedule
.... 4. **out of reach**	d. a passenger boat
.... 5. **troublesome**	e. not enough
.... 6. **ferry**	f. reduce greatly
.... 7. **scenic**	g. an object which is borrowed for a fee
.... 8. **lack of**	h. uneven
.... 9. **slash**	i. inaccessible
.... 10. **choppy**	j. famous in a bad way
.... 11. **notoriously**	k. on the edges
.... 12. **nightmare**	l. difficult

Inside the train ↓↘

Taiwan High Speed Rail

The Taiwan High Speed Rail service has drastically reduced travel times in western Taiwan. Trips between Taipei and Kaohsiung can be completed in less than half the time possible on the regular rail network. Despite this, when the trains began operating in 2007, passenger numbers were far less than had been expected. As time has gone on, however, the service has become more popular.

Food *on the Go*

In Taiwan, especially if you're traveling by train, the most popular kind of food to eat on a journey is the rice box (known locally as "bian dang" 便當). You can buy rice boxes on most trains and in many train stations. They contain rice, obviously, some vegetables, usually half a boiled egg, and some kind of meat—often a pork chop.

Freeways

Taiwan's first freeway was finished in 1978, and runs between Keelung 基隆 and Kaohsiung. Since then, more freeways have been built, but almost all of them are on the western side of the country. Speed limits vary, but they are usually either 100 or 110 kmh.

Air Travel

The Taiwan High Speed Rail service has reduced the popularity of domestic air travel in Taiwan, but thousands of people still fly from place to place within Taiwan every day. There are regular flights between the Taiwanese mainland and outlying islands, and many people fly when traveling from east to west or vice versa. Taiwan's high central mountains mean that cross-country journeys by road or rail are difficult or even impossible. Flying might be more expensive, but it can save a lot of time.

Chapter 7

Traveling in the City

Vocabulary

1 navigate v.
2 problematic a.
3 transit n.
4 invest v.
5 route n.
6 LED abbr. =Light Emitting Diode
7 privacy n.
8 extensive a.
9 terminal n.
10 scooter n.
11 license n.
12 pedal v.

1 An MRT Entrance in Kaohsiung City
2 Taxis line up for passengers outside a mall.

Reading

 21

Traveling from place to place within Taiwan's towns and cities varies in difficulty depending on where you are. The bigger the city, the easier it is to get around. So, while people who don't speak any Chinese shouldn't have too much trouble navigating[1] Taipei, smaller towns might be more problematic[2].

If you're in Taipei, one of the most convenient modes of transport is the MRT (Mass Rapid Transit[3]). The system is wide ranging, extremely clean, and very cheap. Trains stop at many locations around the city and even travel out to tourist destinations such as the Taipei Zoo, Danshui 淡水, and Beitou 北投. Single trips cost between NT$20 and NT$65, but regular travelers can also buy one-day tickets or invest[4] in an EasyCard. This is a stored-value card, and it can be used to pay for MRT, bus, and some train trips in and around Taipei. Many shops, especially convenience stores, and even some taxi drivers will accept payments made with an EasyCard.

Taipei's bus network reaches even more places, and service on most routes[5] runs very regularly. Another great thing about buses in Taipei is that many of them have LED[6] signs that show what the next stop will be in English and Chinese. Fares are usually very low, but some vehicles can get very crowded. If you're unsure about what bus to take or just want a little more comfort and privacy[7], it's easy to get a taxi in Taipei. There are taxis lined up outside most train and MRT stations and many more can be found driving along the busy roads in the city.

Kaohsiung also has an MRT system, and tickets are similar in price to the ones in Taipei. Travelers can buy one-day, two-day, or even 100-day tickets, or they

Taipei's bus network

Renting motorcycles is a good way to travel in Taiwan.

Most streets in Taiwan have English signs.

can purchase the Kaohsiung stored value card, which can also be used on the city's buses and ferries. Kaohsiung's MRT system isn't as extensive[8] as the one in Taipei, but more lines are planned for the future. A lot of buses run through the city, and the main bus terminal[9] is located directly outside the train station.

An MRT system is also being built in central Taiwan's Taichung City 台中市. In fact, the network might eventually stretch to the nearby cities of Changhua 彰化 and Nantou 南投. Bus service here and in other places around the country is not as frequent or well developed as it is in Taipei and Kaohsiung.

People in Taiwan's smaller cities rely on taxis or their own transport. Scooters[10] can be rented in most towns, and rental centers are usually located near train stations. However, you should only ride a scooter if you have a license[11]. If not, a bicycle is a safer option. Cycling is very popular in Taiwan. Even in big cities, people sometimes pedal[12] to school or work. If all else fails, you can always walk. The only problem is that many streets, especially in smaller towns, don't have sidewalks, so be careful!

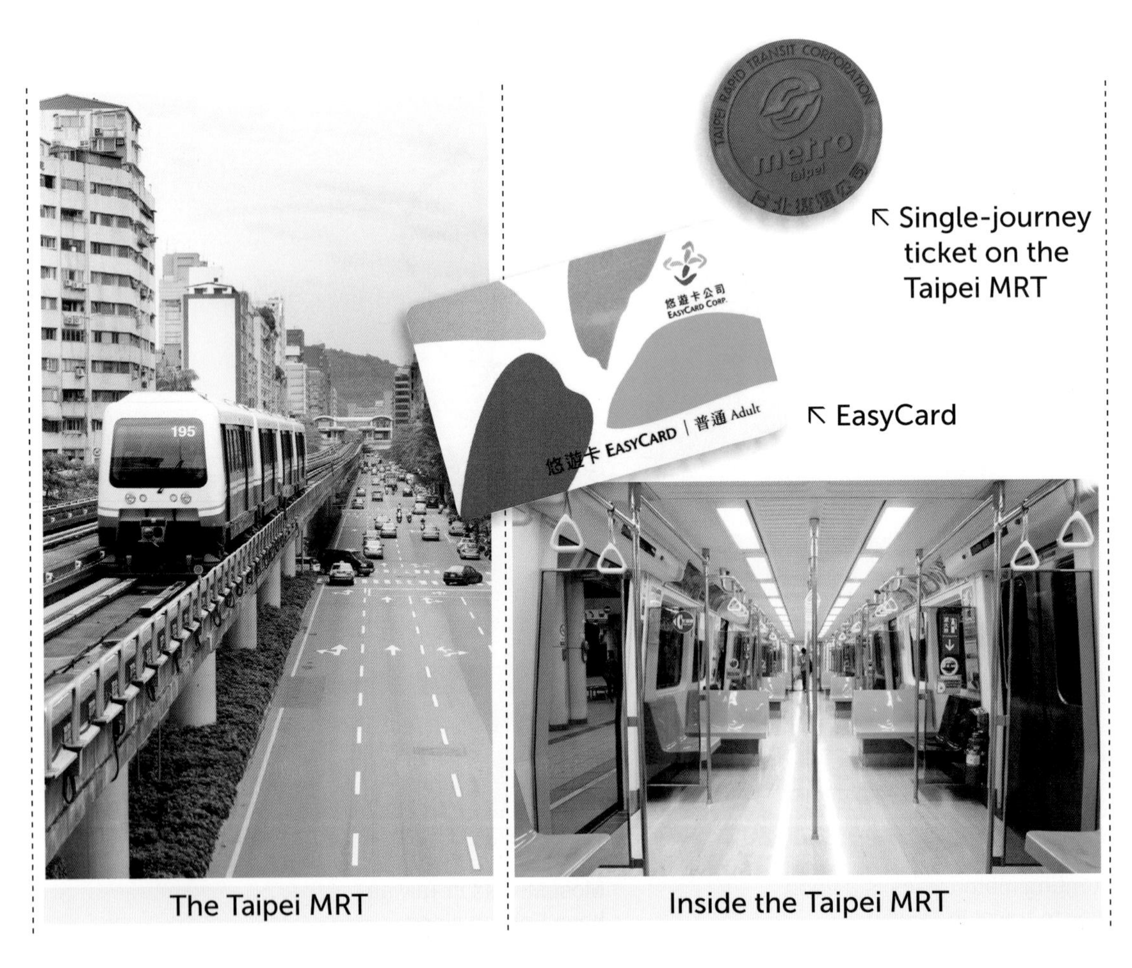

↖ Single-journey ticket on the Taipei MRT

↖ EasyCard

The Taipei MRT

Inside the Taipei MRT

Reading Comprehension

Choose the correct answer based on the Reading.

________ **1. What is the final paragraph mainly about?** (Subject Matter)

ⓐ How to get around Taiwan's smaller cities.
ⓑ The pros and cons of taking the bus.
ⓒ The difference between Taipei's and Kaohsiung's MRTs.
ⓓ The pleasures of cycling in Taiwan.

________ **2. What is given as a bad feature of Taipei's buses?** (Supporting Details)

ⓐ There's often a lot of trash on them.
ⓑ They're slow as they get held up in traffic.
ⓒ It's difficult to know where they're stopping.
ⓓ There can be a lot of people on them.

________ **3. How much do trips on the Kaohsiung MRT likely cost?** (Making Inferences)

ⓐ Between NT$10 and NT$40.
ⓑ Between NT$5 and NT$50.
ⓒ Between NT$20 and NT$80.
ⓓ Between NT$50 and NT$100.

________ **4. What is said in the passage about scooters?** (Supporting Details)

ⓐ You can usually rent them near bus stations.
ⓑ They are extremely easy for people to ride.
ⓒ They are generally quite inexpensive to rent.
ⓓ They should only be used by licensed people.

________ **5. In the first paragraph the writer says that for non-Chinese speakers, traveling in Taiwan's smaller towns can be "problematic." The opposite of "problematic" is ________?** (Antonyms)

ⓐ complex ⓑ straightforward ⓒ tricky ⓓ puzzling

Dialogs

A bus stop by the National Palace Museum

22

Asking for information in the tourist information center about getting to Taipei's National Palace Museum

Tourist	Hi there. I'm really interested in going to the National Palace Museum, but I don't know how to get there. Could you give me directions, please?
Guide	Of course, sir. There are actually a few different ways to get there, but you'll have to take the MRT and a bus whatever you do.
Tourist	That's OK.
Guide	Right, well, you can take the MRT Red Line to Shilin Station 士林站 and then take the "Red 30" bus to the museum.
Tourist	That sounds easy.
Guide	Good. If you're on the MRT Brown Line, however, you should go to either Dazhi Station 大直站 or Jiannan Road 劍南路站 Station. If you go to Dazhi, take the "Brown 13" bus, and if you go to Jiannan Road, take the "Brown 20" bus. They both go right to the museum.
Tourist	That's fantastic. Thank you for your help.

23

Getting around Yuanlin 員林, Changhua County 彰化縣

Molly	Where are you off to tomorrow?
Graham	I'm going to a town called Yuanlin. A friend of mine is in a hospital down there. I've got my train ticket to get there, but I don't know how I'll find my way to the hospital.
Molly	Actually, I used to live in Yuanlin. Maybe I can help.
Graham	Oh, that would be great. Well, my friend is in the Goodness Clinic. Do you know it?
Molly	Yes, and I could draw you a map to get there from the train station, but it's a long way to walk.
Graham	Is there anywhere I could rent a scooter?
Molly	There is, but you might as well take a taxi. It'll be cheaper.
Graham	I guess you're right. Is it easy to find taxis in Yuanlin?
Molly	Yeah, you won't have any problems. There are always a few taxis waiting outside the train station.

Taxis are easily found in most Taiwan cities.

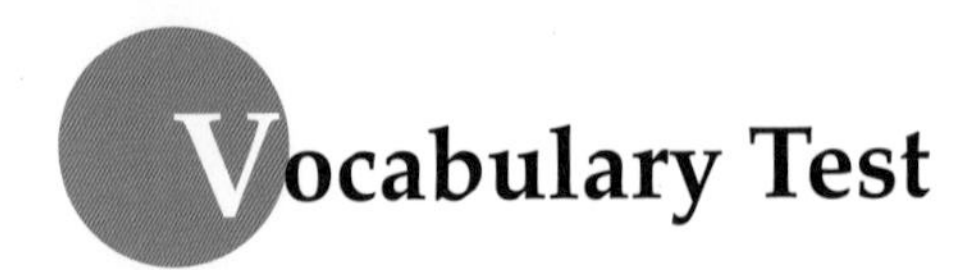

Vocabulary Test

Choose the correct word to complete each sentence.

transit
routes
Navigating
license
terminal
problematic
fares
invented
privacy
extensive
pedaling
scooters

1. ______________ big cities in Taiwan is not difficult for tourists who don't speak Chinese.

2. Getting around Taipei on the MRT is very convenient, especially since someone ______________ the EasyCard, which is a stored-value card.

3. Buses on most ______________ in Taipei have LED signs.

4. If you're tired of public transportation, taxis can offer more comfort and ______________.

5. The Taipei MRT system is ______________, and it is still expanding.

6. In Taiwan's smaller cities, people mostly depend on taxis or ______________ for their daily transportation needs.

7. Taipei Bus Station is the city's main bus ______________, and it was opened on August 19, 2009.

8. People with an international driving ______________ are able to drive a private motor vehicle in this country.

9. In Taiwan, the sight of people ______________ a bicycle to school or work is a common sight.

10. Finding a parking space for a car in a big Taiwanese city can be very ______________.

11. Forms of public ______________ include buses, trains, subways, ferries and even trolleybuses in some cities.

12. Bus ______________ are usually low in Taiwan, and people rely on the bus system for transportation in their daily lives.

More Facts About Taiwan

→ New MRT lines

Taiwan's MRT networks are expanding. In Taipei alone, several new lines and extensions will be opened over the next few years. An extension to Kaohsiung's Red Line is due to be completed in the future, and many new lines have been planned. In both cities, and in Taichung, the MRT lines will spread far and wide and serve millions of people. It seems clear that the MRT is the future of urban transport in Taiwan.

→ Kaohsiung Ferries

Public transport in Kaohsiung includes the Qijin 旗津 Ferry service. The vessels link the district of Qijin, which is an island, to the rest of Kaohsiung. The ferries are mainly used by tourists, as the locals generally drive their cars or scooters through the Qijin Harbor Tunnel. In addition to pedestrians, many cyclists use the ferry, and a few people even drive their scooters on board.

Bus Lanes

Although traffic on Taipei's roads is often quite busy, buses are still a fast form of transport. The reason is that many of the city's busiest roads have special lanes that only buses can drive in. This means that buses are usually on time, even in rush hour.

Bike Rentals

In Taipei and Kaohsiung, people can easily get around using public rental bikes. Rows of public bikes can be found in many places across both cities. For a small price, people can rent the bikes and ride them wherever they want to go. The best thing is that the bikes can be returned to any of the city's bike stations.

Chapter 8 Choosing Accommodation

Vocabulary

1	facilities n. (pl.)	7	spa n.
2	hostel n.	8	lavish a.
3	accommodation n.	9	gorgeous a.
4	spacious a.	10	pricey a.
5	furnish v.	11	extravagantly adv.
6	coastal a.	12	upmarket a.

Reading  24

Once you've gotten to your destination, you'll probably need to find somewhere to stay. That's actually really easy to do in Taiwan, regardless of whereabouts in the country you are. It doesn't even matter what your budget is or what kinds of facilities[1] you require. There's usually something to suit almost everyone. Most hotels and hostels[2] are listed on the Internet, and in larger cities, visitor centers in train or bus stations should be able to give you advice on accommodation[3] in the area.

In Taiwan's biggest cities, you'll find a number of expensive, high-class hotels. You should expect spacious[4], well-furnished[5] rooms, excellent, English-speaking staff, a good breakfast, and possibly a gym. Mid-range hotels are still very nice and, as long as you're not staying in the middle of Taipei or Kaohsiung, shouldn't be too expensive. They should also provide breakfast and things like in-room Internet connections. Budget hotels are easily found in towns and cities, and they can really help travelers keep their costs down. The only problem is that while some places are clean and comfortable, others are definitely not, so make sure you see the room before you pay.

1 Luxurious resort

2 Comfortable "minsu"

3 Uniquely decorated "minsu"

Out in the country, hotel rooms can be just as expensive. In coastal[6] areas like Kenting 墾丁, resort hotels have pools, restaurants, bars, and sometimes even spa[7] facilities. In scenic areas like Sun Moon Lake 日月潭, high rates buy you lavish[8] rooms and gorgeous[9] views of the surrounding landscapes. Hot spring resorts can also be extremely pricey[10]. Not only are they sometimes situated in beautiful locations, but the bathrooms are often extravagantly[11] decorated. Of course, it's not essential to spend a lot of money when you stay in the country, and more reasonably priced hotels with good facilities can be found.

A popular form of accommodation in Taiwan is known locally as "minsu 民宿." They can be big or small, cheap or expensive, but they're all family-owned places where the paying customers live in the same building or complex as the owners. Some of these places are very upmarket[12] and exclusive, but others are more like homestays where you stay in the spare room of somebody's house. The homestay variety offers a less private experience than you would have in a hotel, but it can be a good way to learn a little bit more about local culture and family life in Taiwan.

Backpacker hostels are fairly common in cities and nearby popular tourist destinations. Many offer dorm rooms, shared bathrooms, and very little else, but some of them do have private rooms and higher standards of comfort.

Taiwan also has thousands of motels. You'll generally find them on the edges of urban areas and along major roads throughout the country. They are popular with businesspeople whose jobs might take them out of town. Room rates vary according to where you are and the quality of the motel itself. Rooms are sometimes rented for just a few hours as some motorists want a quick nap rather than an overnight stay.

Rooms are usually ↓ equipped with toiletries.

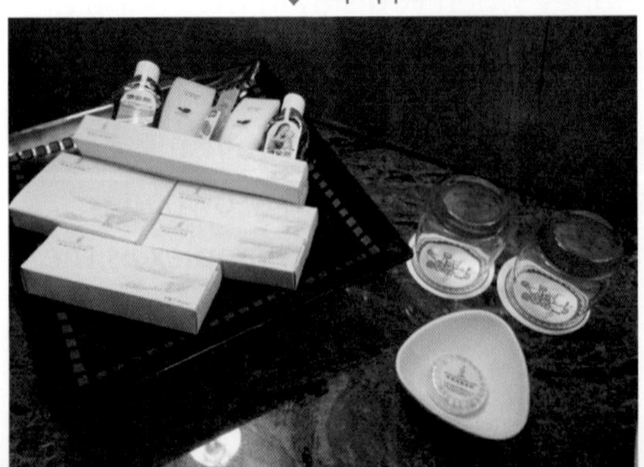

Motel room

Reading Comprehension

Choose the correct answer based on the Reading.

.... **1. The third paragraph focuses on accommodation options ....** (Subject Matter)

ⓐ suited to backpackers
ⓑ in big cities
ⓒ suited to businessmen
ⓓ in rural areas

.... **2. According to the passage, which of the following might you find in one of Taiwan's high-class city hotels?** (Supporting Details)

ⓐ Work-out facilities.
ⓑ KTV facilities.
ⓒ Spa facilities.
ⓓ Cooking facilities.

.... **3. "In scenic areas like Sun Moon Lake, high rates buy you lavish rooms and gorgeous views of the surrounding landscapes." Another word for "lavish" is ....** (Synonyms)

ⓐ cheap
ⓑ moderate
ⓒ barren
ⓓ luxurious

.... **4. According to the passage, where are Taiwan's motels usually located?** (Supporting Details)

ⓐ Near popular sights.
ⓑ Along city boundaries.
ⓒ Next to office blocks.
ⓓ In city centers.

.... **5. What might be the best accommodation option to learn about Taiwanese culture?** (Making Inferences)

ⓐ Backpacker hostels.
ⓑ Motels.
ⓒ Minsus.
ⓓ Resort hotels.

Dialogs

1 vacancy n.
2 coupon n.
3 bureau n.
4 in mind

↑ A Taiwanese-style breakfast is provided in many hotels in Taiwan.

Checking into a mid-range Taichung hotel

Clerk	Hello, sir. Can I help you?
Ken	Yes. I'd like to check in for the night.
Clerk	We've got a few vacancies[1]. What kind of room would you like?
Ken	Just a standard room will be fine.
Clerk	OK, a standard room for one night will be NT$2,400. You can pay when you check out tomorrow.
Ken	Great, what time is checkout?
Clerk	Any time before 12. We also serve breakfast between 7 and 10.
Ken	Is that included in the room fee?
Clerk	Yes, it is. Just take this coupon[2] to the restaurant on the second floor in the morning.
Ken	OK.
Clerk	There's also a gym on the seventh floor. It's open 24 hours a day.
Ken	Excellent.
Clerk	Here's your key. Your room's on the fourth floor, and the elevators are on the left. Enjoy your stay.
Ken	Thanks.

↑ Cheap but cozy and clean hotels are available almost everywhere in Taiwan.

↑ Some motel rooms can be extremely luxurious.

↑ Jacuzzi in a nice hotel room

26

Asking a tourist information **bureau**[3] clerk about accommodation options

Wendy	Hi, I was hoping you could give me some information about accommodation in Taipei.
Clerk	Are you looking for a room for tonight?
Wendy	Yes, I am.
Clerk	What kind of budget do you have?
Wendy	I don't have a fixed amount of money in mind[4]. I've never stayed in Taipei before, and I don't know how much things cost.
Clerk	OK, so what kind of hotel are you looking for?
Wendy	I'm looking for something cheap, actually. I want my own room, and I want it to be clean, but apart from that, I don't really mind.
Clerk	OK. That should be pretty easy. You'll find budget hotels all over the city, and you should expect to pay between NT$1,000 and NT$1,500 dollars a night.
Wendy	That sounds encouraging. I'm going to be meeting a friend by the Zhongxiao Dunhua 忠孝敦化 MRT Station. Are there any hotels near there?
Clerk	Yeah, there are a lot of hotels in that area. However, the room rate is a little higher there.

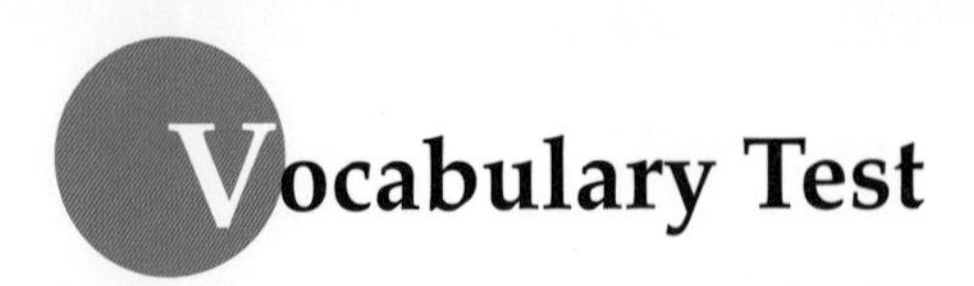

Vocabulary Test

Choose the correct word to complete each sentence.

- facilities
- lavish
- upmarket
- accommodation
- in mind
- gorgeous
- furnished
- vacancies
- coastal
- spacious
- coupon
- extravagantly

1. Five-star hotels are usually equipped with leisure ____________, such as fitness centers, spas, indoor heated pools and even hairdressing salons.
2. Before you visit a foreign country, you could go online to check out ____________ options.
3. If you are traveling on a budget, you might not be able to afford big and ____________ rooms.
4. Most of the hotels provide ____________ rooms, breakfast, and an Internet connection.
5. Kenting National Park is located in Taiwan's southern ____________ area and is well known for its tropical climate and sunshine.
6. If you have lots of money to spend, ____________ rooms are available.
7. From the top of the tall building, you'll get ____________ views of the surrounding landscapes.
8. The rooms in this expensive hotel are all ____________ decorated.
9. The new department store offers ____________ services and goods designed for wealthy people.
10. The hotel rooms are all booked. There are no ____________ left.
11. You can use this ____________ to get a free cup of coffee.
12. I don't have a fixed amount of money ____________. I've never been to this restaurant.

Camping

Taiwan's generally good weather means that it is the perfect place to go camping. Campsites can be found all around the country, and many have excellent facilities. In addition to showers with hot water, some sites even have electrical outlets for each camping plot. Some Taiwanese people have lots of camping equipment and even cook huge meals in the evenings.

Cooking on Your Own

At some hostels both in the country and city, and at a few popular tourist destinations, you can find accommodation with kitchen facilities. In hostels, this might mean you'll have use of a communal kitchen, but out in the country, there are many places where you can rent small holiday cottages with a full kitchen or kitchenette.

Temples, Schools, and Police Stations

When you're out in the country, it's possible to camp out next to police stations and schools. If you don't have a tent, some schools and temples will even let you sleep inside the buildings. Amazingly, you won't even be expected to pay for your night's rest.

The Lalu Hotel 涵碧樓

Its position as Taiwan's most expensive hotel might have been taken in the past few years by luxury hotels in Taipei, but the Lalu is still one of the most luxurious on the island. It was built on the banks of Sun Moon Lake and rooms have great views across the water. There's also a spa, a pool, a gym, and a sauna. A one-night stay in the smallest room in the hotel can cost over NT$15,000.

Unit 3 Food and Beverages

27

Taiwanese cuisine has developed over hundreds of years and has been influenced by the country's unique geography and history. Taiwan is a small, mountainous island, so there isn't a huge amount of land available for farming. Throughout history, people have therefore cooked up whatever foods they could **get hold of**[1]. As a result, the ingredients used in modern Taiwanese dishes are extremely varied. They also include a few things that might not be eaten in other parts of the world. Since Taiwan's history is so closely connected with China's, food here also has a distinct Chinese flavor.

Taiwanese people are pretty **obsessed**[2] with food, **so much so that**[3] when they greet each other in Taiwanese, they often ask "have you eaten?" This **fixation**[4] with food includes a desire to try as many flavors as possible, and it might be the reason why there are so many different types of snacks here. These range from Western foods like fried chicken to traditional Chinese dim sum, and of course there are Taiwanese snacks as well. Some of these **delicacies**[5] look, taste, and smell like nothing you have ever come across before. Their names—stinky tofu and 100-year-old eggs for example—might **put** some people **off**[6] trying them, but be brave and give them a go because they actually have incredible flavors.

The Taiwanese also have a real sweet tooth[7], and desserts and sugary drinks are very popular here. Drink stores where you can buy juices, teas, and sodas are a very common sight, and the drinks they serve are sometimes packed with sugary syrups. Sweet puddings and cakes are also popular here, and many regions and cities around the country are known for a particular kind of cake or candy. All this talk of sugar and pudding shouldn't give you the impression[8] that Taiwanese food is unhealthy. A lot of the sweet foods eaten here are made with fresh fruit, and many local dishes also make use of an amazing variety of vegetables.

As Taiwan is a fairly small island, a lot of seafood is eaten here. People seem to eat any living thing that comes out of the sea. You'll find all kinds of fish in all different sizes and colors, and many other kinds of sea creatures as well. Seaweed is also a common ingredient in many foods—it's even sometimes used as a flavoring. Some of the other flavors you'll often taste in Taiwan are soy sauce, garlic, ginger, chili pepper, and sesame oil. Herbs, spices, sauces, wines, and strong-tasting foods are also used to make local dishes taste delicious.

Taiwan is a food lover's paradise[9], and the best part about it is that you can buy meals and snacks almost anywhere you go and at almost any time of day or night. Food stalls, cafés, and restaurants fill the roads in any built-up area. Many of them are open very late, and breakfast stores start serving food before dawn. All in all[10], it's impossible to go hungry in Taiwan!

1 get hold of
2 obsessed a.
3 so much so that
4 fixation n.
5 delicacy n.
6 put . . . off
7 sweet tooth
8 impression n.
9 paradise n.
10 all in all

Chapter 9 Taiwanese Cooking and Ingredients

↑ Deep-fried stinky tofu

Vocabulary

1 stir-fry v.
2 deep-fry v.
3 griddle v.
4 spit n.
5 texture n.
6 ingredient n.
7 protein n.
8 banquet n.
9 shellfish n.
10 consume v.
11 intestine n.
12 cultivation n.
13 herb n.
14 garnish v.
15 cilantro n.

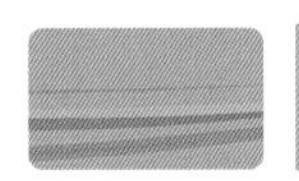

Reading

28

To get a great introduction to Taiwanese cuisine, just walk around a night market. You'll find them in practically every town and city around the country, and they're full of people cooking lots of different foods in lots of different ways.

In many parts of the world, people prepare the majority of their food using only a couple of cooking methods. But in Taiwan, things work very differently. People here use an incredible variety of cooking methods. Travel around the country and you'll see dishes being steamed, boiled, stir-fried[1], deep-fried[2], barbecued, griddled[3], roasted in clay ovens, or rotating on spits[4]. The different forms of cooking produce different flavors and textures[5], but an even more important aspect of Taiwanese cooking lies in the ingredients people use.

By far the most important ingredient[6] in Taiwan is rice. Tons of it are eaten every year, and some people even have it as a part of all three daily meals. The popularity of rice is declining, though, as more and more people are choosing noodles instead.

↑ Fish market

↑ Stir-fried clams with basil

Surrounded by the sea, Taiwan has always relied on seafood. Almost everyone in Taiwan, both rich and poor, enjoys seafood. Cheaper items provide many people with an important source of protein[7], while more expensive kinds of seafood are often served during extravagant banquets[8]. As well as a wide range of fish and shellfish[9] such as crab, lobster, and shrimp, the Taiwanese eat octopus and squid. And the local love of seafood doesn't stop there. Seaweed is also eaten here as a vegetable or a snack and is also sometimes used to flavor dishes.

All different kinds of meats are consumed[10] in Taiwan, although pork is probably the most popular. Traditionally, beef was not commonly eaten here. This is because oxen and water buffalo were used on most farms, and farmers had a strong attachment to these hard-working animals. But, as the farming industry has declined, the consumption of beef has increased. Beef can now be found in shops everywhere alongside chicken, goat, and duck. What you'll also see on the supermarket shelves is a wide range of animal products including liver and intestines[11]. In addition to all that, some indigenous people still hunt, and they eat whatever they catch.

Taiwan has a great selection of both fruits and vegetables. Its tropical climate is perfect for the cultivation[12] of many kinds of fruits including bananas, pineapples, and mangoes. The Taiwanese also eat a diverse selection of leafy and root vegetables.

Many local dishes are heavily flavored with sauces, herbs[13], and spices. Soy sauce, rice wine, ginger, and garlic are the most frequently used flavorings, and many Taiwanese people add chili peppers or chili sauce to their meals to give them extra heat. Food is also often garnished[14] with herbs such as basil and cilantro[15], pickled white radish, spring onions, and even dried fish.

These ingredients have helped Taiwan cuisine become rich and varied. With so many flavors to be tried, it should come as no surprise to find that food plays a central role here.

↙ Bok Choy

↙ Water bamboo

Bananas ↓

Reading Comprehension

Choose the correct answer based on the Reading.

_______ **1. What's the main idea of paragraph four?** (Main Idea)

- ⓐ Seafood is an important source of protein for many Taiwanese.
- ⓑ The most expensive seafood is served during banquets.
- ⓒ Seaweed is sometimes used to flavor dishes.
- ⓓ Seafood has always been a big part of the Taiwanese diet.

_______ **2. What is said in the passage about cooking methods?** (Supporting Details)

- ⓐ Some methods are unique to Taiwan.
- ⓑ Taiwanese people use a lot of them.
- ⓒ Taiwanese people use more than anyone else.
- ⓓ Many of them were actually invented in Taiwan.

_______ **3. What, most likely, is the author's view of Taiwanese food?** (Making Inferences)

- ⓐ It's very diverse.
- ⓑ It's not very nice.
- ⓒ It's very healthy.
- ⓓ It's very simple.

_______ **4. "What you'll also see on the supermarket shelves is a wide range of animal products including liver and intestines." "Intestines" are most likely a kind of _______.** (Words in Context)

- ⓐ musical instrument
- ⓑ organ meat
- ⓒ TV show
- ⓓ traditional clothing

_______ **5. Which of the following is listed as one of the most frequently used flavorings?** (Supporting Details)

- ⓐ Cilantro.
- ⓑ Seaweed.
- ⓒ Garlic.
- ⓓ Chili.

Dialogs

1 boiled a.
2 start off
3 pour v.
4 grab v.

29

Talking about the favorite kinds of food

Gary	Hey, do you want to come to the night market with me?
Kim	Yeah, sure. That sounds like fun.
Gary	What sort of food do you like to eat?
Kim	I really like to buy barbecued foods when I go to the night market.
Gary	I don't really like that. I prefer to buy deep-fried duck.
Kim	Urrgghh! I hate eating duck, although I do like deep-fried chicken.
Gary	Me, too. And I think I'm going to get a few steamed buns as well.
Kim	Mmm, nice. I would do the same, except that I had buns for lunch.
Gary	So, what do you think you will get?
Kim	I'm not sure. Maybe some noodles, although I don't know if I want them fried or served with **boiled**[1] vegetables.
Gary	That's a tough decision.
Kim	Yeah, but it's also a tasty one. Come on, let's go. I'm hungry!

↓ Braised pork rice 滷肉飯

↑ Deep-fried chicken 鹽酥雞

Steamed buns 包子 ↘

30

Talking about a special kind of soup

Neil	That soup looks really interesting. What's in it?
Rachel	A lot of things, actually.
Neil	Yeah, like what?
Rachel	To **start off**[2] with, there are a lot of vegetables, including carrots, bamboo shoots, mushrooms, and onions.
Neil	Any meat?
Rachel	There's a bit of pork, and there's some tofu, too.
Neil	It looks like you've got some noodles in there.
Rachel	Yeah, that's right, although you can have it without.
Neil	Would you ever put rice in there?
Rachel	I suppose you could, but I've never seen anyone do it.
Neil	And what's that you're adding to it now?
Rachel	Oh, I'm just **pouring**[3] in some sesame oil and a little bit of pepper in order to give it some more flavor.
Neil	Wow, I'm guessing it's a really tasty soup.
Rachel	Why don't you try some for yourself?
Neil	OK, I'll just **grab**[4] another spoon.

Hot and sour soup
酸辣湯 →

Vocabulary Test

Choose the correct word to complete each sentence.

- spits
- herbs
- Stir-fried
- protein
- Shellfish
- deep-fried
- cultivation
- textures
- ingredients
- intestines
- banquet
- consumed

1. ____________ cabbage with chili is a very common Taiwanese dish.
2. In many countries around the world, people love ____________ food.
3. In most night markets in Taiwan, you can see vendors barbecuing meat on ____________.
4. Different forms of cooking produce different flavors and ____________.
5. In Taiwanese cuisine, green onions, ginger, and garlic are important ____________.
6. Soybeans are a cheap but significant source of ____________.
7. It's tradition in Taiwan that when a couple gets married, they have a big wedding ____________.
8. ____________, such as crab, lobster, and shrimp, is one kind of food that my friend Alice never gets tired of.
9. Among all the meats ____________ in Taiwan, pork is probably the most popular.
10. A lot of westerners are not fans of eating animal ____________, such as liver, lungs, and heart.
11. Rice ____________ is in decline on this island.
12. This dish needs a pinch of ____________ to enrich its flavor.

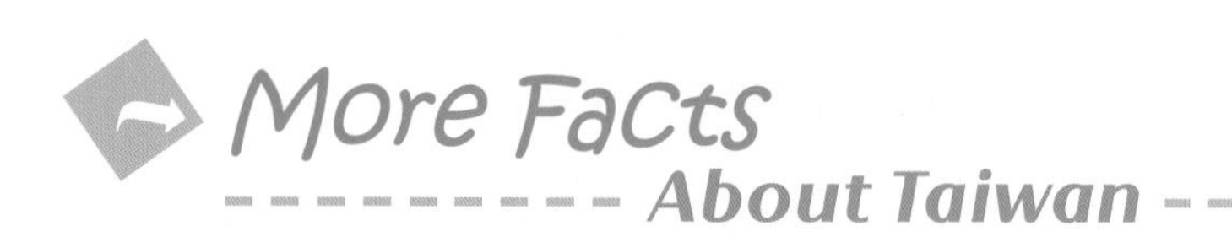

Taiwanese rice

Taiwanese farmers and scientists have worked hard to produce superior varieties of rice. One of the most popular kinds is called Yi Chuan Aromatic rice 益全香米. This rice is short and quite sticky, which makes it easier to eat with chopsticks. In Western countries, longer, drier varieties of rice are usually preferred.

Sweet potatoes

The Taiwanese are very inventive with their food, and they use sweet potatoes in a few different ways. They're used as a vegetable, in place of rice or noodles as a staple food, and sometimes as a flavoring. Instead of using sugar to sweeten foods, sweet potato is sometimes added as a healthy sweetener.

Tofu

Tofu is a very important ingredient in Taiwanese cooking. The influence of Buddhism means that many people in the country are vegetarians. Others simply want a cheaper, healthier form of protein than meat. In addition to soft, white tofu, you can also buy dou gan 豆乾 and dou pi 豆皮. Dou gan is much drier and harder than tofu—the "gan" part of its name comes from the Chinese word for "dry." Dou pi is created by taking the skin off the top of pots of boiling soy milk. The skin is then cooled and dried.

Red yeast rice

These are purple-red grains, and they're created by adding a certain type of mold to rice. Grains of red yeast rice are used to give color to a wide variety of different foods and drinks. The ingredient also leaves food with a nice, mild flavor. Cookies with this flavor can now be bought in most supermarkets and convenience stores.

cc by FotoosVanRobin

Chapter 10 Local Snacks

Preserved eggs 皮蛋

Duck tongues 鴨舌頭

Tea egg 茶葉蛋

Ice cream spring roll with peanuts 花生捲冰淇淋

Vocabulary

1. vendor n.
2. stall n.
3. skewer v.
4. catch one's eye
5. braise v.
6. gravy n.
7. stinky a.
8. scent n.
9. ferment v.
10. pickled a.
11. omelet n.
12. starch n.
13. soak v.
14. appearance n.
15. transform v.

Reading 31

The Taiwanese love to eat. It's a passion that means dinners can be very large and contain many different dishes. It also means that Taiwan is home to a wonderful range of snacks, or "xiao chi" 小吃 (literally "small eat"). These little tasty treats are available almost everywhere—you'll find them in night markets and convenience stores, and there are usually lines of vendors[1] selling them at the country's larger tourist attractions.

Many of these snacks, like fried chicken, appear ordinary enough, but others will give some foreign tourists a bit of a shock. In fact, if you take a closer look at that fried chicken stall[2], you might see a few unusual items on sale. Next to the legs, wings, and slices of chicken breast, it's not uncommon to see chicken feet, strips of curled up skin, or even four or five chicken bottoms skewered[3] onto a wooden stick.

Another kind of deep-fried food that might catch your eye[4] is duck. You might even see a few eyes in the stall, since duck head is one of the most popular items. The heads, including the beak, are braised[5] in soy sauce gravy[6], then deep-fried, before being served to customers. If a whole head sounds like it might be too much for you, you might want to try something smaller, like a few duck tongues.

Moving on from snacks that look interesting, it's time to discuss one that has an interesting smell: stinky[7] tofu 臭豆腐. This is one food that you'll definitely smell before you see, as it has an incredibly powerful scent[8]. It's made by fermenting[9] tofu in saltwater, and a range of different flavorings. It can be left in the liquid for as long as a few months and is then cooked by steaming or deep-frying. It has a very creamy flavor and texture, and those who love the food say you shouldn't be put off by the smell. It's sometimes served with pickled[10] vegetables and chili sauce.

A lot less smelly, but just as tasty, is the oyster omelet[11] 蚵仔煎. It uses eggs that are thickened with potato starch[12], and, in addition to oysters, it usually contains green, leafy vegetables. Cooked omelets are topped with generous quantities of salty, spicy, or sweet sauces.

Eggs are cooked and prepared in many different ways to create tasty Taiwanese snacks. The most common is the tea egg 茶葉蛋, which you'll find at snack stalls and in convenience stores around Taiwan. These hard-boiled eggs are soaked[13] in water flavored with spices, sauces, and tea leaves.

Preserved, or 100-year-old eggs 皮蛋, have a more unusual appearance[14] and flavor. They're covered in clay, ash, salt, and a few other things. The chemicals in these ingredients turn the egg yolks a grey-green color and the whites are transformed[15] into a brown jelly. The colors and smells of these eggs might make a lot of people turn away, but, like stinky tofu, preserved eggs actually have a smooth, creamy flavor.

↑ Deep-fried chicken bottoms

↑ Stinky tofu

↑ Oyster omelet

↑ Taiwanese meatball
肉圓

↑ Black pepper cake
胡椒餅

↑ Stewed food
滷味

Local Snacks

↖ Pig's blood cake
豬血糕

↑ Mixed vegetable roll
潤餅捲

↑ Salty chicken
鹽水雞

↑ Danzi noodles
擔仔麵

↑ Rice tube pudding
筒仔米糕

↑ Barbecue
碳烤

↑ Grilled corn
烤玉米

Reading Comprehension

Choose the correct answer based on the Reading.

______ 1. **According to the passage, how are duck heads cooked?** (Supporting Details)

ⓐ They are slowly cooked in gravy and then deep-fried.
ⓑ They are roasted in a clay oven and then slowly boiled.
ⓒ They are steamed and then quickly barbecued.
ⓓ They are stir-fried and then quickly griddled.

______ 2. **What part of the chicken is described in the passage as being unusual?** (Supporting Details)

ⓐ The breast.
ⓑ The tongue.
ⓒ The insides.
ⓓ The feet.

______ 3. **Throughout the passage, a lot of focus is given to ______.** (Subject Matter)

ⓐ the price of each snack
ⓑ how each snack is made
ⓒ the history of each snack
ⓓ how healthy each snack is

______ 4. **The article is arranged as ______.** (Clarifying Devices)

ⓐ a series of causes and effects
ⓑ a problem and a solution
ⓒ a series of examples
ⓓ a series of questions and answers

______ 5. **The author says that stinky tofu "has an incredibly powerful scent." A synonym for "scent" is ______.** (Synonyms)

ⓐ taste ⓑ smell ⓒ sound ⓓ texture

Tsong you bing (green onion pancake) 蔥油餅

Dialogs

1 pancake n.
2 filling n.
3 hollow v.

32

Discussing a popular kind of snack

Diana	What's that you're eating? It looks good.
Ethan	Um, I don't know if it's got an English name, but we call it "tsong you bing" 蔥油餅.
Diana	"Tsong you bing," huh? It looks a bit like a thick pancake[1].
Ethan	I guess you could say that. The outside part of it is made from flour and water, and then they add green onions to give it a bit of extra flavor.
Diana	What else have you got in there?
Ethan	I've got an egg, and you can also choose all different kinds of fillings[2].
Diana	Yeah? Could I have bacon?
Ethan	You could. That's a pretty popular choice actually. You could also get pork, ham, cheese, and cabbage.
Diana	I think I'm going to try one. Where can I get one from?
Ethan	There's a vendor selling them over there. That's where I got this one from.

33

Asking about coffin sandwiches

Tourist	I'm going to be in Tainan later this week, and I was just wondering if there are any foods that I should try while I'm down there?
Guide	Hmm, let me think . . . Tainan is actually famous for shrimp rolls.
Tourist	Oh, I've already tried them. They're great, but is there anything else?
Guide	You could also try a coffin sandwich.
Tourist	That sounds interesting. What is it exactly?
Guide	It's a very thick piece of toasted bread that has been **hollowed**[3] out and then filled with a sort of thick soup.
Tourist	OK, what kinds of things would be put into the sandwich?
Guide	It's usually seafood, carrots and some other vegetables, chicken or pork, and sometimes liver. Flour or potato starch is mixed with water and milk to make the soup.
Tourist	I think I'll give that a try. Thanks for the information.
Guide	You're welcome. Happy eating!

Shrimp rolls ↗
蝦捲

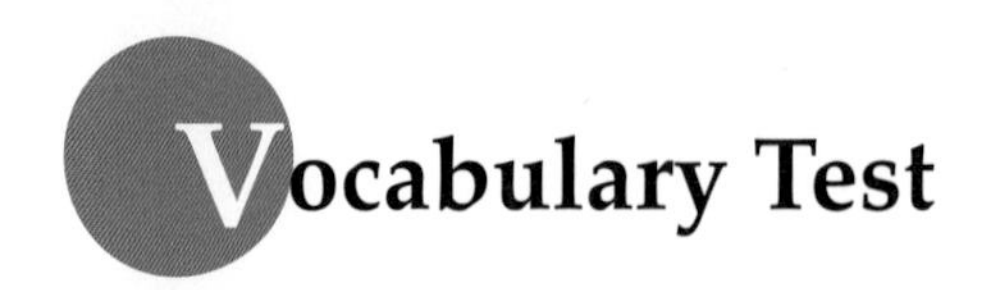

Vocabulary Test

Choose the correct word to complete each sentence.

- vendors
- ferment
- hollow
- skewered
- appearance
- stinky
- stall
- omelet
- fillings
- scent
- pickled
- gravy

1. In summer, ______________ will sell different tropical fruits on the streets in Taiwan.
2. Every time I go to the night market, I have to go to the chicken ______________ to buy some chicken feet and wings.
3. My dad ______________ three to four chicken bottoms onto wooden sticks for the barbecue.
4. After you finish the turkey, you can dip bread into the ______________. It tastes great!
5. You have to wash your feet more. Otherwise, your feet are going to be ______________.
6. When the candle was lit, a beautiful ______________ filled the room.
7. I remember when I was little, my grandmother used to ______________ grape wine in the summer.
8. The ______________ vegetables should be served cold from the fridge.
9. Nowadays, due to the economic recession, you won't find too many oysters in an oyster ______________.
10. Preserved eggs have an interesting ______________, and the white area is almost transparent.
11. Dumplings have various different ______________, including pork, shrimp, cabbage, and even cheese.
12. First, you'll have to ______________ out the bread and put seafood and cheese in it. After that, you put it in the oven for 10 minutes.

More Facts
About Taiwan

Sausages

Sausages are popular all over the world, but they taste a little different in Taiwan. They're usually a little sweet, and they're sometimes made with strong rice wine. Meat sausages are often served with larger sausages made from rice. Some people also like to eat them with raw garlic.

Oyster noodles 蚵仔麵線

Oysters aren't just used for oyster omelets. Another popular use for the shellfish is oyster noodles. The noodles used in this snack are very thin, the soup is very thick, and the oysters are very juicy. Oyster noodles are often garnished with cilantro.

Flavored nuts

For a really small snack, you might want to try some nuts. There's a wide selection available in Taiwan. Cashew nuts are often coated in sugar and honey. There are also almonds that have been mixed with small, salty fish. For something spicier, you could try peanuts that have been coated in wasabi.

Chips

Chips may not have been invented in Taiwan, but Taiwanese people love eating them. As a result, there are lots of flavors, including chili sauce and squid, that you won't find in many other countries. Not only that, but chips are also made with some unusual ingredients like peas.

Seaweed

Strips of dried seaweed are eaten by many people as a tasty snack. There are many different flavors including salt, sesame oil, and wasabi. Seaweed is actually enjoyed all over East Asia, and flavors from other countries can be found in Taiwan. One of the most popular flavors is kimchi, which is a kind of preserved cabbage from South Korea.

Chapter 11 Chinese Cuisine in Taiwan

Reading 34

Chinese culture influences just about every aspect of life in Taiwan, and food is no exception. Chinese restaurants can be found all over the country, and many of them are extremely popular. Trying to describe Chinese cuisine is difficult, though, as it's so wide-ranging. The reason for this is that China is a massive country, and it has deserts, mountainous areas, and coastal regions. Its population incorporates[1] people from many different cultural backgrounds as well. The food eaten in one place is therefore very different than the food found somewhere else. The good news is that if you want to try it all, you don't have to travel all around China, because all the contrasting[2] cooking styles and flavors can be sampled in Taiwan.

Huaiyang 淮揚 cuisine is one of the most influential in China, and it originates[3] from Jiangsu Province 江蘇省 in the east. Dishes are very carefully prepared, and they are known for having delicate[4] flavors. Pork and seafood caught in the nearby Huai 淮河 and Yangtze Rivers 揚子江 provide the foundations[5] for the cuisine. This style of food generally has a mildly sweet flavor, and powerful spices like chili peppers are rarely used. One of the most popular dishes is noodles with pork and shrimp dumplings.

Vocabulary

1. incorporate v.
2. contrasting a.
3. originate v.
4. delicate a.
5. foundation n.
6. rounded a.
7. organ n.
8. a lot more to
9. aromatic a.
10. intense a.
11. be packed with
12. shallot n.
13. cure v.
14. authentic a.

↗ Gong Bao chicken 宮保雞丁

Cantonese cuisine, from southern Guangdong Province 廣東省, is probably the most well-known form of Chinese food in the West. Sauces, spices, garlic, and ginger are used to give Cantonese dishes rounded[6] flavors. Sweet and sour pork 咕咾肉 is a great example of how contrasting ingredients are used together in a single dish. This form of cooking also makes use of a wide range of meats and internal organs[7].

Sichuan 四川 cuisine is famous for being spicy, but there's a lot more to[8] this food than just heat. In addition to hot spices, various Sichuan dishes make use of sour, sweet, bitter, aromatic[9], and salty flavorings. Whatever ingredients are used, however, the taste of the final dish will almost always be intense[10]. Beef is more common in Sichuan cooking than in other Chinese cuisines due to the large number of cows in this southwest region. Despite that, the most famous Sichuan dish is probably Gong Bao Chicken 宮保雞丁.

Hunan 湖南 cuisine is generally packed with[11] chili peppers, garlic, and shallots[12]—ingredients that give the food an incredible heat. Dishes make use of a wide range of ingredients, including a lot of cured[13] and smoked meats. One of the most interesting aspects of Hunan cooking is that people eat very different foods in the summer and winter. When it's hot, people eat cold cuts of meat and chili peppers, as this is supposed to cool you down. In the winter, hot pot is preferred.

Since Beijing is the capital city of China, it has attracted many of the country's top chefs. As a result, its cuisine has been influenced by the cooking styles of other regions. The most authentic[14] Beijing foods are the small snacks that can be found in the city. Popular flavorings include soy paste, sesame paste and oil, and spring onions. The city used to be called Peking in the West, and that name lives on in the region's most famous dish: Peking Duck 北京烤鴨.

Yuanyang hot pot 鴛鴦鍋

Sliced pork with garlic sauce 蒜泥白肉

Home-style fried tofu 家常豆腐

Chicken soup 雞湯

Mapo tofu 麻婆豆腐

Stir-fried vegetables 炒青菜

Reading Comprehension

Choose the correct answer based on the Reading.

_____ **1. Why is it probably better to eat Chinese cuisine in Taiwan rather than in China?** (Making Inferences)

ⓐ The food served in China is no longer made traditionally.
ⓑ The different kinds of cuisine can be found in a small place.
ⓒ All of the best Chinese chefs moved to Taiwan years ago.
ⓓ The ingredients in Taiwan are of higher quality than those in China.

_____ **2. What is the main idea expressed in paragraph four?** (Main Idea)

ⓐ There's more to Sichuan cuisine than hot spices and Gong Bao Chicken.
ⓑ Beef is more common in Sichuan cuisine than in other Chinese cuisines.
ⓒ Sichuan cuisine is known for its intense, and often very spicy, flavors.
ⓓ Gong Bao Chicken is probably the most famous of Sichuan's many dishes.

_____ **3. What is said about Beijing cuisine?** (Supporting Details)

ⓐ It's the most well-known form of Chinese food in the West.
ⓑ It is the healthiest of China's different cuisines.
ⓒ It uses a lot of spicy ingredients.
ⓓ It contains elements of other cooking styles.

_____ **4. "Sauces, spices, garlic, and ginger are used to give Cantonese dishes rounded flavors." The word "rounded" in this context probably means _____.** (Words in Context)

ⓐ curved ⓑ smooth-edged ⓒ well-developed ⓓ fleshy

_____ **5. According to the passage, what is special about Hunan cuisine?** (Supporting Details)

ⓐ It's eaten by almost everyone all across China.
ⓑ Different things are served in different seasons.
ⓒ It has a longer history than any of the other cuisines.
ⓓ It is the most expensive form of Chinese food.

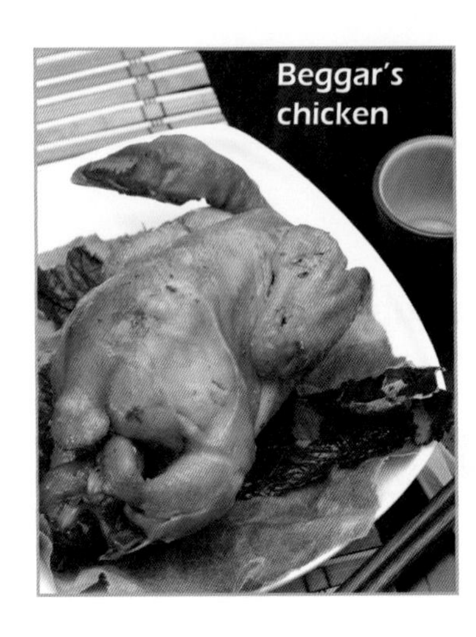

Dialogs

35

Talking about Chinese food

Jane	I can't wait to go on holiday to China. It should be great.
Ben	What are you looking forward to the most?
Jane	All the food I'm going to eat. I love Chinese food.
Ben	What kind of Chinese food are you talking about?
Jane	I don't really know what you mean.
Ben	Well, there are many kinds of Chinese food, and some taste different than others.
Jane	Oh right, I didn't know. I just like the stuff I get in my local Chinese restaurant in Italy. I usually order sweet and sour pork and wonton soup.
Ben	That sounds like Cantonese food to me. It comes from the southern region of Guangdong. Since you're going to Beijing, the food might be a bit different.
Jane	Oh! Never mind. It should be fun to try something new. Is there anything you recommend?
Ben	Try Beggar's Chicken 叫化子雞. It's really tasty.

Chili peppers, garlic, and Sichuan pepper are commonly used in Chinese cooking.

36

Talking about which restaurant to go to for dinner

Michael	What would you like for dinner tonight?
Yvonne	I was thinking about something spicy. Are there any good restaurants around with really hot food?
Michael	What about that Sichuan place in the middle of town?
Yvonne	It closed down about a month ago.
Michael	Oh dear. I liked it there. What other kinds of Chinese food are spicy?
Yvonne	The spiciest I know of is Hunan food.
Michael	I don't think I've ever eaten it. Is it good?
Yvonne	That depends on whether you like chili peppers or not. Hunan chefs use lots of them in almost everything they cook.
Michael	You know I love spicy food. Is there a Hunan restaurant near here?
Yvonne	I'm just checking on the Internet. . . . Apparently, there's a new place on the other side of town. Shall I call and book us a table?
Michael	Definitely. All this food talk is making me really hungry!

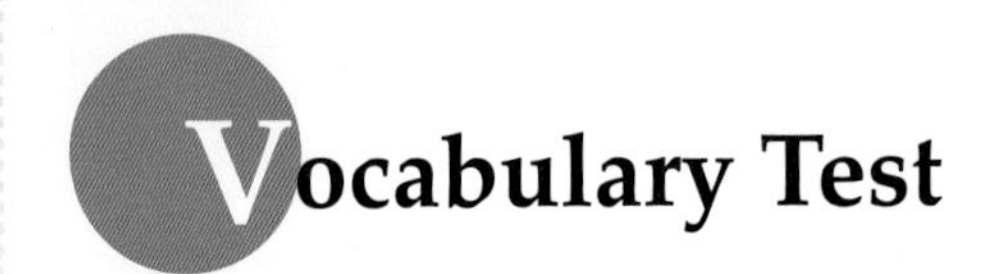

Vocabulary Test

Choose the correct word(s) to complete each sentence.

- authentic
- intense
- a lot more
- delicate
- contrasting
- originates
- cured
- packed
- aromatic
- shallots
- foundation
- incorporates

1. Chinese cuisine ________________ food from many different regions and backgrounds.
2. Dim sum is a style of Cantonese food that ________________ from Guangdong province in China.
3. A lot of Japanese food is prepared in a very ________________ way.
4. The ________________ of being a good chef is understanding what ingredients work well with each other.
5. Sichuan dishes are famous for their sour, sweet, bitter, ________________, and salty flavorings.
6. Authentic tom yum soup in Thailand has a very ________________ flavor, which is not for everyone.
7. Chili peppers, garlic, and ________________ are the basic ingredients in Hunan cuisine.
8. Preserved meat, which is ________________ and smoked, is a very traditional Chinese food.
9. If you want to try ________________, local food, this restaurant is great place to go.
10. A Thanksgiving turkey is sometimes ________________ with walnuts, chopped onions, celery, salt, and freshly ground pepper.
11. Even though Taiwan is a small island, it's home to many ________________ cooking styles.
12. There is ________________ to Chinese cuisine than fried rice and spicy food. There are actually a wide variety of dishes.

More Facts About Taiwan

Lion's head meatball 獅子頭

This is a popular dish in Huaiyang cuisine. The meatballs are very large—sometimes as big as 10 centimeters across—and they're usually served in a watery soup. They're made with pork and sometimes contain some vegetables. Because of their size, they are said to resemble lions' heads.

Cha shao pork 叉燒肉

This red-colored, barbecued pork dish is famous around the world. It's a Cantonese dish, and its name can be literally translated as "fork burn." Before the meat is placed onto a fork to be "burnt," it's coated with a brightly-colored, strong-tasting sauce. This sauce contains many ingredients including honey, soy sauce, rice wine, and five spice.

Tea-smoked duck 樟茶鴨

This Sichuan dish doesn't contain any chili. Instead, a whole duck is covered with Sichuan chili peppers, garlic, ginger, and salt and then left for a few hours. It's then quickly boiled before being smoked over tea leaves. To finish off the cooking process, the bird is briefly deep-fried.

Braised pork 紅燒肉

This Hunan dish was a favorite of former Chinese leader Mao Zedong 毛澤東. Thick pieces of pork—complete with fat and skin—are stewed in a mixture of water, soy sauce, bean paste, darkened sugar, and spices. This leaves the meat with a reddish color and a beautiful flavor. Braised meat is also usually soft and juicy.

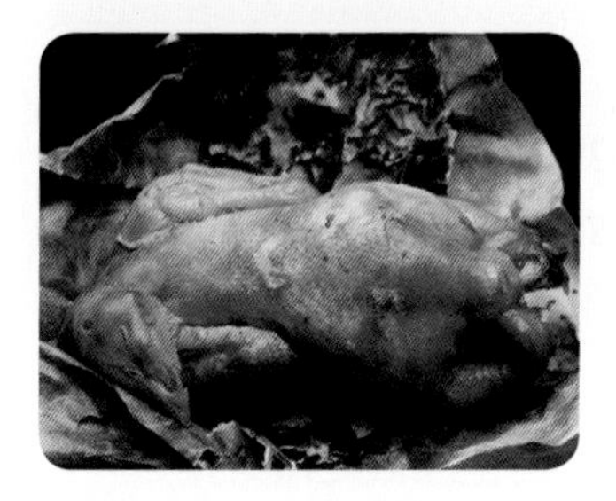

Beggar's chicken 叫化子雞

According to some stories, a poor man once stole a chicken and buried it in mud so he wouldn't be caught. He later cooked it while it was still covered in mud. When he peeled off the hard, dry mud, the meat underneath was wonderfully juicy. Cooking beggar's chicken is more complicated now, but it's still coated in clay before it's cooked.

Chapter 12

The Most Important Meal of the Day

↑ Radish cake 蘿蔔糕

Reading

 37

Breakfast is big business in Taiwan. Shops and stalls selling breakfast and lunch items are a regular sight in both the largest cities and the smallest towns. They open their shutters[1] early in the morning and are typically[2] closed for the day by lunchtime.

One of the most popular items is the "dan bing" 蛋餅. It's a kind of pancake that contains eggs and possibly some other filling, as well. The round pancake is lightly fried and then rolled up and cut into small pieces. Popular fillings for "dan bing" are bacon, tuna, corn, and cheese, and they're usually served with thick soy sauce or chili sauce.

Another breakfast favorite is the hamburger. They're sometimes made with beef, but pork, bacon, and chicken are far more conventional[3]. Breakfast hamburgers usually contain a fried egg, lettuce, tomato, and cucumber, so they're not quite as unhealthy as the burgers served at fast food restaurants.

Sandwiches are also popular, and you'll actually find them for sale in most convenience stores. In breakfast stores, pre-packaged sandwiches can usually be seen lined up[4] on the counter. They'll be made with cold ingredients like cheese,

Vocabulary

1 shutter n.
2 typically adv.
3 conventional a.
4 line up
5 diameter n.
6 mince v.
7 taro n.
8 layer n.
9 diner n.
10 squeeze v.
11 congee n.
12 supplement v.
13 give it a try

↑ Bao zi (steamed buns) 包子

↑ Fan tuan (rice roll) 飯糰

ham, dried pork, and salad vegetables. Hot sandwiches can be made to order, and they contain the same ingredients that are put in hamburgers. Breakfast stores also make a variety of fried foods including noodles, radish cake, chicken nuggets, and dumplings.

In more traditional breakfast stores, you'll get a different selection of foods. Some of the most common things are steamed bread buns. Some of them, called "bao zi" 包子, contain a filling, while others, "man tou" 饅頭, do not, but both kinds are about 8-10 centimeters in diameter[5]. Typical fillings for "bao zi" include minced[6] pork, cabbage, leeks, red bean, or taro[7]. Although "man tou" do not contain tasty foods, they are sometimes flavored with taro or cocoa. Some people eat them as they are, but others like to cut them open and pack them with fried eggs, ham, bacon, and other kinds of typical breakfast foods.

Another traditional breakfast food is the "fan tuan" 飯糰, which literally means "rice roll." To make them, a layer[8] of cooked rice is spread out on a thin piece of plastic. Diners[9] can then choose what goes inside, but some of the most common selections are dried pork, eggs, and pickled and dried vegetables. The rice is then rolled up and squeezed[10] together, trapping the fillings inside.

Congee[11] is another popular breakfast dish, but you won't often see it being sold on the streets. It's far more common for people to eat it in their own homes, and most hotels that provide breakfast for their guests serve congee. Congee can be made either thick or watery, and it can be supplemented[12] by almost any kind of food you can think of. In most hotels, you'll see dishes of dried pork, eggs, cabbage, and a few other kinds of vegetables next to the congee. It might look unusual to Westerners, but everyone should give it a try[13]—they might be pleasantly surprised.

Cold noodles 涼麵

Congee

Sandwiches

Fried dumplings 煎餃

Toast with strawberry jam

Clay oven roll with fried bread sticks 燒餅油條

Hamburger

Reading Comprehension

Choose the correct answer based on the Reading.

_____ **1. Another title for the article could be _____.**
(Subject Matter)

ⓐ The Classic Sandwich ⓑ A Breakfast Feast
ⓒ Time for Tea ⓓ Food on the Go

_____ **2. What does the writer probably think about congee?**
(Making Inferences)

ⓐ It's a tasty dish. ⓑ It's not very nice.
ⓒ It looks appealing. ⓓ It is unhealthy.

_____ **3. According to the passage, which of the following is NOT true about breakfast hamburgers?**
(Supporting Details)

ⓐ They're healthier than those found in fast food restaurants.
ⓑ They usually contain a fried egg as well as a burger.
ⓒ They're most commonly made with beef.
ⓓ They're one of the most popular breakfast foods.

_____ **4. Breakfast stores "open their shutters early in the morning and are typically closed for the day by lunchtime." "Typically" means _____.**
(Words in Context)

ⓐ energetically ⓑ sweetly
ⓒ rarely ⓓ normally

_____ **5. What is said in the passage about congee?**
(Supporting Details)

ⓐ It's available in almost every breakfast store.
ⓑ It's only sold in traditional breakfast stores.
ⓒ It's more often eaten at home than in stores.
ⓓ It's the most popular breakfast food in Taiwan.

Dialogs

1 pop v.
2 muffin n.
3 fluffy a.

Hamburger with bacon 培根漢堡

38

Talking about the breakfast store

Stacy	Do you want to come with me to the breakfast store?
Paul	Yeah, sure. I'm feeling pretty hungry actually.
Stacy	What do you think you'll order?
Paul	Hmm, I'm not sure. I usually just get two bacon dan bing, but I'm going to get something else today. What will you order?
Stacy	I'm going to have some noodles with an Italian-style meat sauce.
Paul	That sounds good, but I had noodles last night and I want something different.
Stacy	How about a hamburger?
Paul	Yeah, I could do that. I'll order one with pork, bacon, and egg.
Stacy	Tasty.
Paul	Yeah, hopefully. I think I'll order some fried dumplings as well.
Stacy	Seriously? That's so much food. Are you sure you can finish it all?
Paul	Oh yeah, definitely. My day doesn't feel right unless I start it with a big breakfast.

Man tou (steamed Chinese buns) 饅頭

Bacon and corn dan bing 培根玉米蛋餅

Noodles with Italian-style meat sauce 義大利肉醬麵

39

Having food at a traditional breakfast store

Phil	Good morning, Wendy. Have you eaten breakfast yet?
Wendy	No, I was going to **pop**[1] into the fast food restaurant and get a **muffin**[2].
Phil	Forget about that. Come with me to a traditional Taiwanese breakfast store instead.
Wendy	Is the food there good?
Phil	Of course. I go there almost every morning for my breakfast.
Wendy	OK, I suppose I could give it a try.
Phil	You won't regret it.
Wendy	So what kind of food can I get there?
Phil	I usually get a fried egg and cheese in a man tou—that's a steamed Chinese bun.
Wendy	OK. What else do they have?
Phil	They make a really good rice roll. It's basically a big ball of rice filled with tasty things like dried vegetables, pickles, and dried pork.
Wendy	Dried pork? Do you mean that **fluffy**[3] orange stuff?
Phil	That's the stuff.
Wendy	Uggh, I hate it. I think I'll have a man tou like you.

Vocabulary Test

Match the words with the correct definitions.

....	1.	give it a try
....	2.	shutters
....	3.	taro
....	4.	conventional
....	5.	diameter
....	6.	lined up
....	7.	supplemented
....	8.	diner
....	9.	layer
....	10.	congee
....	11.	typically
....	12.	minced

- a. a sheet of some material
- b. rice porridge
- c. in a row
- d. to be improved by adding something else
- e. metal barrier that covers shop or house entrances
- f. someone who is eating
- g. usually
- h. sample something
- i. a root vegetable
- j. cut into very small pieces
- k. a line running across a circle
- l. common

More Facts
About Taiwan

Dried pork 肉鬆

This food is sometimes called pork floss, and it has a fluffy, wool-like texture. It's made by boiling pork in soy sauce until the meat can be pulled apart into its separate fibers. After that's done, the meat is dried by cooking it in a huge wok, or Chinese frying pan. Dried pork has a slightly sweet flavor, and it's used in many breakfast foods.

Soy bean milk

This kind of milk is a lot more popular here than it is in the West. It's drunk both hot and cold and is often given to children. Although soy bean milk is healthier than cow's milk in that it doesn't contain much fat, it's common in Taiwan to sweeten the drink with large amounts of sugar.

Cereal

Despite the trend for Western breakfasts, cereal is still not very popular in Taiwan. You can buy most kinds of cereal in the supermarkets. There are obviously some health-conscious people here, because you can usually find a good selection of muesli and oatmeal on the supermarket shelves.

Western-style brunch stores

Western-style breakfast and brunch stores are becoming increasingly popular in Taiwan. They usually sell Taiwanese breakfast foods as well as a few European options. Along with omelets, you might find cold cuts of meat and salad. These stores are usually healthier and more expensive than regular breakfast stores.

Chapter 13 Oodles of Noodles and Dim Sum

Beef noodles

Vocabulary

1 be split into
2 annual a.
3 consist of
4 essential a.
5 version n.
6 vermicelli n.
7 chewy a.
8 minimal a.
9 stewed a.
10 dim sum
11 portion n.
12 combination n.
13 vinegar n.

Star anise ↘

Reading 40

There are literally hundreds of different ways to serve noodles, but they can be split into[1] three main categories: soup noodles, fried noodles, and dry noodles. Probably the best-known noodle dish in Taiwan is beef noodles. In fact, it's so well loved that there's even an annual[2] Beef Noodle Festival in Taipei. At the event, chefs from around the country compete to see who can cook the best bowl of this tasty food. The dish consists of[3] noodles and usually some form of leafy vegetable in a heavily flavored beef soup. Surprisingly, actual pieces of beef are not an essential[4] part of the meal, and many people order a version[5] of the dish without any meat. The soup is usually seasoned with soy sauce and spices like star anise.

Oyster vermicelli[6] 蚵仔麵線 is another much-loved soup noodle dish. The soup is thickened with corn flour and flavored with fresh shellfish. Unlike Italian vermicelli, the noodles are very thin, and they're steamed, which makes them chewy[7] and gives them a golden brown color. Other kinds of soup noodles are made with little dumplings, or wontons, and also with meat, seafood, and vegetables. Instant noodles are also incredibly popular, and most of them come with their own soup flavorings.

A meal of fried noodles might not sound very healthy, but they often contain a lot of vegetables and a minimal[8] amount of oil. A typical dish is made with strips of meat, carrots, cabbage, onions, and mushrooms and is flavored with garlic and soy sauce or Chinese barbecue sauce.

Although dry noodles can be made with any kind of meat or vegetable, they're generally mixed with little pieces of stewed[9] pork, boiled bean sprouts, and leeks. Slices of pork, sesame oil, and garlic are sometimes added to make the dish more interesting.

Oyster vermicelli 蚵仔麵線 | Noodles with seafood 海鮮麵 | Fried noodles 炒麵

Dry noodles 乾麵 | Fried rice noodles 炒米粉 | Instant noodles 泡麵

Dim sum[10] 點心 basically consists of small dishes prepared in separate, individual portions[11], and many of them are served to restaurant diners in traditional bamboo baskets that are used for steaming. Small buns, dumplings, rolls, soups, cakes, and some of the foods introduced in Chapter 10 can all be described as dim sum.

Steamed dumplings can be filled with meat (usually pork), shrimp, or vegetables. Some of them even contain a little soup. They taste delicious, but you have to be careful as the soup inside is very hot. Taiwanese people like to dip their dumplings in sauce before eating them. Everyone makes their dipping sauce differently using a combination[12] of soy sauce, chili peppers or sauce, sesame oil, vinegar[13], garlic, ginger, and spring onion.

Most Westerners have come across spring rolls 春捲. They're little flour and water pancakes filled with thinly sliced vegetables, meat, and mung bean noodles. Once they've been rolled up, they're deep-fried and served with sauce. Larger and thicker pancakes are used to create much larger rolls. These ones are filled with sliced meat and spring onions and then cut into pieces.

Reading Comprehension

Choose the correct answer based on the Reading.

.... 1. **In the first paragraph, the author uses the word "surprisingly" to indicate ....** (Clarifying Devices)

ⓐ an unexpected relationship
ⓑ a shocking fact
ⓒ a statistic that dispels a common belief
ⓓ an unpredicted outcome

.... 2. **The first four paragraphs focus on ....** (Subject Matter)

ⓐ the three main types of noodle dish
ⓑ how noodles are made
ⓒ why noodles are better than rice
ⓓ the history of beef noodles

.... 3. **Spring rolls need to be fried, rolled, dipped in sauce, and filled, but in what order?** (Sequencing)

ⓐ They are rolled, dipped in sauce, fried, and filled.
ⓑ They are filled, rolled, dipped in sauce, and fried.
ⓒ They are filled, rolled, fried, and dipped in sauce.
ⓓ They are rolled, filled, fried, and dipped in sauce.

.... 4. **"Dim sum basically consists of small dishes prepared in separate, individual portions." In this sentence, a "portion" is most likely a(n) ....** (Words in Contexts)

ⓐ large field filled with flowers
ⓑ pen used for holding farm animals
ⓒ device used to measure temperature
ⓓ amount of food suitable for one person

.... 5. **What is said about fried noodles?** (Supporting Details)

ⓐ They are not really healthy.
ⓑ They could be called dim sum.
ⓒ They are flavored with vinegar.
ⓓ They often include meat.

Dialogs

41

Dining in a dim sum restaurant

Mel	I don't know what I'm going to order. There's so much on the menu.
Nikki	Yeah, that's how it works at dim sum restaurants. Don't worry, though. The portions are quite small, so you can order a lot of different things.
Mel	That's good to know. I think I'll get some dumplings, some spring rolls, and some radish cake.
Nikki	OK. What kind of dumplings do you want? I want to get some leek dumplings and also some with pork and shrimp.
Mel	Nice. I think I'll get the pork and cabbage dumplings and a beef roll . . . and something else . . . . Are you getting the radish cake with shrimp and mushroom?
Nikki	I was going to, yes.
Mel	Can I share it with you?
Nikki	Of course you can.
Mel	Great! Why don't we order? Er, waiter . . .

Siu mai
燒賣

Spring rolls
春捲

Dumplings with shrimp
蝦餃

42

Talking about noodles

Tourist	It seems like all the convenience stores sell instant noodles.
Tour guide	They do. Many people here love to eat them.
Tourist	Are they good? The ones we get in Germany are terrible.
Tour guide	I don't eat them very often because they're not really healthy, but they do taste good.
Tourist	Do you eat other kinds of noodles?
Tour guide	Oh yes. There's a stall near my house that serves beautiful dry noodles.
Tourist	Dry noodles? Does that mean there's a dish called wet noodles?
Tour guide	Ha ha, not quite, but noodles often come in soup. Dry noodles just have a bit of sauce on them.
Tourist	Interesting. Is there anything that you would recommend that I try while I'm in Taiwan?
Tour guide	You should try beef noodles. It's practically a national dish.
Tourist	OK, I'll do that. Thanks.

Barbecued pork buns
叉燒包

Rice meat balls
珍珠丸

Chicken feet
鳳爪

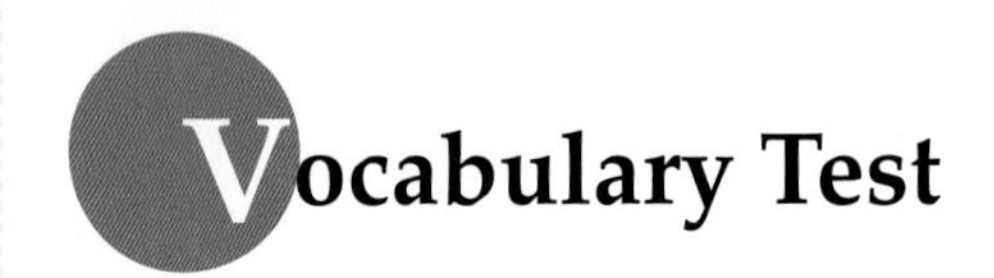

Vocabulary Test

Choose the correct word(s) to complete each sentence.

- essential
- portions
- vermicelli
- vinegar
- combination
- chewy
- stewed
- consisted of
- oodles
- minimal

1. My grandmother's signature dish—pearl meat balls— ______ the best glutinous rice and fatty pork meat.
2. Soybean sauce is an ______ ingredient in Taiwanese cuisine.
3. Oyster ______ is one of the most famous night market dishes in Taiwan.
4. It would be healthier if you used a ______ amount of oil when cooking your food.
5. I loved the ______ chicken my mom used to make when I was little.
6. Lisa likes her food to be served in small ______ so that she can try more things.
7. When we have a hot pot, Dad always likes to make his special sauce, which is a ______ of egg yolk, shallots, soybean sauce, and a little bit of sesame oil.
8. It is supposed to be good for your health if you have a small amount of ______ every day.
9. You'll find ______ of dishes when you go to an all-you-can-eat buffet.
10. The gelatinous dough of ba-wan, or Taiwanese meatballs, is made of sweet potato starch, which is very ______.

Din Tai Fung 鼎泰豐

This is Taiwan's most famous dim sum restaurant. In fact, its food is so well loved that there are now several restaurants in Taiwan and many more around the world. It specializes in steamed buns and dumplings, and the restaurants also serve excellent soup, noodles, and fried rice dishes. At some of the restaurants, it's possible to see cooks preparing the dumplings.

Lotus leaf wraps 荷葉飯

This is a popular Shanghai dim sum dish. A very sticky kind of rice is mixed with chicken, mushrooms, sausage, and spring onions. All of that is wrapped in lotus leaves and steamed. The cooked rice sticks together to form a single, solid piece of food. It might be tempting to just bite into it, but most people prefer to use chopsticks.

Mung bean noodles 冬粉

Not all noodles are made from wheat. One variety is made with rice, and another uses mung beans. They're used in the same way as regular noodles, but they have a different texture and appearance. Bean noodles are chewy and see through. They're also a lot healthier than ordinary wheat noodles.

A world of noodles

Noodles from other Asian countries are also regularly eaten here. Korean instant noodles, called "ramyeon," 拉麵 can now be found in many Taiwanese stores, and Japanese noodles have also become popular. One of the most interesting kinds is called "udon" 烏龍麵 in Japan but "oolong" in Taiwan. They're much thicker and firmer than regular noodles, but, despite the name, they're not connected to oolong tea.

↙ Udon

Pineapple cake

Chapter 14

Desserts and Beverages

Vocabulary

1 beverage n.
2 in truth
3 built-up a.
4 tapioca n.
5 syrup n.
6 condensed a.
7 topping n.
8 variation n.
9 appealing a.
10 almond n.
11 ginger n.
12 pastry n.
13 crumbly a.
14 exterior n.

Reading

43

Western desserts and sweet treats can all easily be found in Taiwan, but most people here prefer locally made cakes, puddings, and beverages[1]. In truth[2], it's not hard to see why people love them as they're tasty, inexpensive, and widely available.

Finding something good to drink is never much of a problem in Taiwan, as there are drink stores on practically every block in built-up[3] areas. The beverages at these places are almost always mixed by hand, and most of them involve tea. There are green teas, black teas, oolong teas, fruit teas, and milk teas. One of the most popular drinks is called pearl milk tea, which is packed with chewy, sweet, little balls, or "pearls," made from tapioca[4] starch. Although this drink is delicious, it's also extremely unhealthy. Fortunately, when you go to drink stores, you can ask for your drink to be made with less sugar.

Another popular Taiwanese drink is grass jelly tea. Lumps of grass jelly, which is made from a mint-like plant, are mixed with syrup[5] and sucked up through a straw. The cooling, minty flavors of the jelly mean that this beverage is especially popular in the hot summer months.

Something else that's sure to cool people down is shaved ice. Bowls are filled with mountains of finely shaved ice and then covered with syrup, condensed[6] milk, and some toppings[7]. Chunks of fresh fruit are a popular choice of topping, and mango seems to be many people's favorite. Kiwi, strawberry, watermelon, and banana are also usually available.

Grass jelly tea 仙草茶

Shaved ice with strawberries, condensed milk, and pudding toppings 草莓牛奶布丁冰

Egg yolk cake 蛋黃酥

Pearl milk tea ↗

Dou hua (tofu pudding) 豆花

Shaved ice with red bean and condensed milk 紅豆牛奶冰

Suncake 太陽餅

Jelly figs 愛玉

Red bean cake 車輪餅

For a variation[8], milk ice is sometimes used for this dish. Not only does this give a different flavor, but it also provides a different texture, since shaved milk ice is much finer. While pieces of fruit would be quite appealing[9] to many Westerners, other popular toppings might seem more unusual. A lot of people like to eat their ice with taro, sweet potato, and red and green beans. These ingredients are actually used in quite a few Taiwanese desserts, and tourists who try them out might be surprised by how much they like them.

Shaved ice is sometimes mixed with tofu pudding, or "dou hua" 豆花, as it's known locally. This is a very soft kind of tofu, and it can be mixed with beans, peanuts, or tapioca pearls. Tofu pudding is also regularly flavored with an almond[10] or ginger[11] syrup, and in the winter, it's usually heated up and served as a warm dessert.

Many kinds of traditional cakes are made around Taiwan, although many of them would be described as pastries[12] in the West. The crumbly[13] exteriors[14] contain sweet, dry fillings that are made from things like sugar, fruit, beans, or vegetables. Others, however, make use of slightly more unusual fillings like dried pork or egg yolk. One of the best known cakes is suncake, which comes from Taichung 台中.

There are so many desserts available in Taiwan, it's impossible to write about them all. Just get out there and start eating. You'll definitely find something that you love.

Reading Comprehension

Choose the correct answer based on the Reading.

.... **1. What is said about Taiwanese desserts and drinks?** (Supporting Details)

ⓐ They all taste very strange.
ⓑ They are often unhealthy.
ⓒ They cost a lot of money.
ⓓ They are all easy to buy.

.... **2. According to the passage, how does shaved milk ice compare to ordinary shaved ice?** (Supporting Details)

ⓐ It has a finer texture.
ⓑ It has a weaker flavor.
ⓒ It doesn't melt as fast.
ⓓ It's less expensive.

.... **3. The final paragraph is intended to ....** (Clarifying Devices)

ⓐ give the reader a lasting impression of Taiwanese desserts
ⓑ give a brief summary of Taiwanese desserts
ⓒ encourage the reader to try Taiwanese desserts
ⓓ warn the reader to stay away from Taiwanese desserts

.... **4. An appropriate subheading for paragraphs two and three would be ....** (Subject Matter)

ⓐ popular drinks ⓑ shaved ice
ⓒ traditional cakes ⓓ pearl milk tea

.... **5. Which of the following has the same meaning as the phrase "in truth" in the first paragraph?** (Synonyms)

ⓐ Back and forth. ⓑ As a matter of fact.
ⓒ By all means. ⓓ On the whole.

Dialogs

1 hazelnut n.
2 amount n.

44

Ordering a beverage at a drinks store

Tourist	So what different kinds of drinks do you have here?
Clerk	There's a menu up there that you can look at, but basically, there are teas, coffees, juices, and sodas.
Tourist	Wow, that's great! The coffee looks good, especially the **hazelnut**[1] latte, but I think I should probably save that for another time. If I drink it now, I'll never sleep tonight.
Clerk	Why not have some tea? That shouldn't keep you awake.
Tourist	OK, I think I will. This one looks interesting, the passion fruit green tea.
Clerk	Good choice, that's my favorite drink, actually.
Tourist	Can I get some ice in that?
Clerk	Of course you can. Do you want a lot of ice or just a little?
Tourist	Just a little, I think.
Clerk	And how much sugar would you like?
Tourist	I don't understand.
Clerk	Well, you can have the full **amount**[2], half sugar, a little sugar, or no sugar.
Tourist	Um, half sugar, please.

45

Talking about eating shaved ice

Heidi	That was a nice dinner.
Jack	Yeah, it was, but now I feel like dessert.
Heidi	That would be good. What would you like?
Jack	How about some shaved ice? There's a great store near here.
Heidi	I don't know. I had it one time and didn't really like it.
Jack	What topping did you have?
Heidi	Mango, but that wasn't the problem. I thought the pieces of ice were too big.
Jack	Have you ever tried milk ice?
Heidi	No.
Jack	You might like it. It has a much finer texture.
Heidi	OK. I'll try it.
Jack	And then you can have chocolate sauce on it. I know you'll like that.
Heidi	You know me well. What will you have?
Jack	I want to get peanuts and taro balls. Mmm, it'll be delicious! I hope you like the milk ice.
Heidi	Well, if I don't, I'm sure you can finish it for me.

Shaved ice with mangoes and condensed milk
芒果牛奶冰

↑ Glutinous sesame balls
芝麻球

Vocabulary Test

Match the words with the correct definitions.

.... 1. **condensed**

.... 2. **built-up**

.... 3. **almond**

.... 4. **syrup**

.... 5. **beverages**

.... 6. **ginger**

.... 7. **in truth**

.... 8. **crumbly**

.... 9. **tapioca**

.... 10. **pastries**

.... 11. **topping**

.... 12. **exteriors**

a. easily broken apart
b. a food that goes on top of something else
c. to be honest
d. made thicker
e. the outsides
f. things you drink
g. a certain kind of nut
h. describing a place that has lots of buildings
i. a kind of fragile, dry cake
j. a root with a very strong flavor
k. a kind of starch made from the cassava plant
l. a sweet liquid

More Facts
About Taiwan

Mochi 麻糬

This glutinous rice snack might have come from Japan originally, but the Taiwanese have made it their own. It is a chewy treat made from rice flour and water, and it comes in a number of different flavors. Some of the most popular fillings are peanuts, sesame, and red and green beans.

Cow tongue cake 牛舌餅

This cake is made in Yilan 宜蘭. It gets its unusual name from its appearance, as it really does look like a long tongue. The thin, oval-shaped pastries are quite dry, and they usually come in milk, sesame, and caramel flavors.

Egg tart 蛋塔

Europeans will be familiar with these tasty little snacks as they're very similar to the British custard tart or Portuguese egg tart. Taiwanese egg tarts are small pastry crusts filled with egg custard. Ingredients like caramel and honey are sometimes added to them.

Tang yuan 湯圓

Tang yuan are little round balls made from rice flour. They're sometimes filled with peanut powder, bean paste, or sesame paste, but they're also occasionally served plain. In Taiwan, they're eaten on shaved ice or in a sweet soup that can be served either hot or cold.

Yang le duo 養樂多

"Yang le duo" is the local name for a kind of milk drink that contains bacteria that is supposed to improve your health by helping you digest your food better. Many drink stores use "yang le duo" to make special beverages. Sometimes they will mix it with green tea or fruit juices. Lemon juice with "yang le duo" is also particularly popular.

Unit 4

Shopping Experience

46

If you enjoy shopping, you'll love Taiwan. **No matter**[1] what you like to buy, no matter how you like to buy it, you should find something that's perfect for you. There are lavish department stores with designer **boutiques**[2]. There are traditional, old-fashioned shopping streets where you can find out what Taiwan used to be like and buy a few things that you wouldn't find in **contemporary**[3] stores. And there are **lively**[4] night markets with vendors selling all kinds of products—often at **bargain**[5] prices.

There's a large connection between food and shopping in this country. Whether you're walking along a shopping street or around a department store, you'll definitely see lots of places to stop and get **a bite to eat**[6]. This could be because people here are always thinking about food, or it might be that many shopping trips last long enough to make dinner or lunch breaks necessary. Whatever the reason, the connection is probably most obvious at night markets. Among all the stalls selling clothes, toys, and household items, you'll see numerous vendors selling food and beverages.

Many things in Taiwan are an incredible combination of ancient and modern elements. The country's shops are no exception. There are shopping districts, like Xinyi 信義 in Taipei, where almost every store sells the latest fashions or electronics. The nation is on the **cutting edge**[7] of computer and electronic **device**[8] technology, so all the latest gadgets can be found here. New shopping developments are also constantly being built in Taiwan. In Kaohsiung, you'll find the Dream Mall 夢時代購物中心, which is one of Asia's biggest department stores, and E-Da World 義大世界, a massive complex that includes a large retail area.

Not everything is new, though, and the Taiwanese love visiting old shopping streets. Walking down one of these streets is a bit like taking a step back into history. The buildings have either been **preserved**[9] or carefully **restored**[10] and the store owners often sell things like traditional clothing and foods. These streets can be found in towns and cities all over the country, and they're almost always popular tourist attractions.

Classic Taiwanese goods are popular with both young and old people. Stores selling Chinese medicine and tea are common sights throughout the country and can be interesting places for tourists to visit. When talking about classic products, it would be impossible not to mention food and wine. Millions of dollars are spent every year on tasty traditional cakes and snacks. Several different kinds of interesting wines are made in Taiwan, and adults are advised to give them a try.

Of course, not everyone in Taiwan is crazy about shopping, and there are a lot of people who want to buy what they need as quickly and cheaply as possible. Night markets can be **ideal**[11] for people like this, and there are also some large stores with huge ranges of items for sale.

All in all, Taiwanese shoppers can enjoy an incredible amount of variety.

---

1 no matter
2 boutique n.
3 contemporary a.
4 lively a.
5 bargain a.
6 a bite to eat
7 cutting edge
8 device n.
9 preserve v.
10 restore v.
11 ideal a.

Chapter 15 Famous Shopping Areas

Vocabulary

1. rival v.
2. given that
3. agricultural a.
4. consumerism n.
5. gadget n.
6. retail a.
7. dominate v.
8. majestic a.
9. luxury a.
10. pedestrian n.
11. handicraft n.
12. accessory n.
13. outlet n.
14. hang out

Reading

47

If there's one thing that can rival[1] Taiwanese people's love of food, it's their love of shopping. Given that[2] Taiwan was a mostly agricultural[3] society 60 years ago, it's incredible how important consumerism[4] has become. Shopping can almost be counted as a national pastime, and many people spend a lot of money buying all the latest clothes and gadgets[5]. Because shopping is so popular, the country's biggest and brightest retail[6] districts have become very well known.

The Xinyi District 信義區 is located in the middle of Taipei, and it must be one of the best shopping districts in the world. The area is dominated[7] by the

Taipei 101 building. It may not be the tallest building in the world anymore, but it's still a majestic[8] symbol of Taiwan's economic success. The massive building also sits right next to a large department store. There's actually a very good choice of department stores in Xinyi, and they all contain shops, cafés, and restaurants. This district is definitely the best place to go if you want to buy luxury[9] goods and designer clothing. As well as all the shops, the Xinyi District has a movie theater and lots of street performers, so you'll have a good time even if you don't buy anything.

If Xinyi has the luxury goods, then Ximending 西門町 is the place to go for youth culture. The district was first developed by the Japanese as an area for entertainment. A couple of the buildings constructed during that period are still standing. The most famous one is probably The Red House 西門紅樓, which was built in 1908. The Ximending shopping area is for pedestrians[10] only, and it always seems to be full of people. The district has hundreds of small clothing stores where you'll find the latest fashions on sale. There are also a few movie theaters and loads of great places to eat.

In central Taichung, the most interesting place to shop is probably Jingming 1st Street 精明一街. Like Ximending, it's a pedestrianized area, so no cars are allowed. Jingming 1st Street is famous for its European-style café culture. Cafés along the street have outdoor seating sections, which gives the area a wonderful atmosphere. To add to the fun, there are often musical performances and street entertainers here. And, of course, there are also some great shops. The stores along Jingming 1st Street sell clothes, jewelry, artworks, and **handicrafts**[11].

Taipei 101

The Shinkuchan Shopping District 新堀江商圈 in Kaohsiung is quite similar to Ximending, as it is a place for youth culture. All the latest Taiwanese, Japanese, and Western fashions can be found in the neighborhood. There are also shops selling the latest electronic gadgets, watches, jewelry, and **accessories**[12]. No Taiwanese shopping area would be complete without a wide selection of food **outlets**[13], and Shinkuchan contains a lot of Western and Japanese fast food stores. For entertainment, you could head to one of the movie theaters or just **hang out**[14] in the noisy, brightly lit, crowded streets.

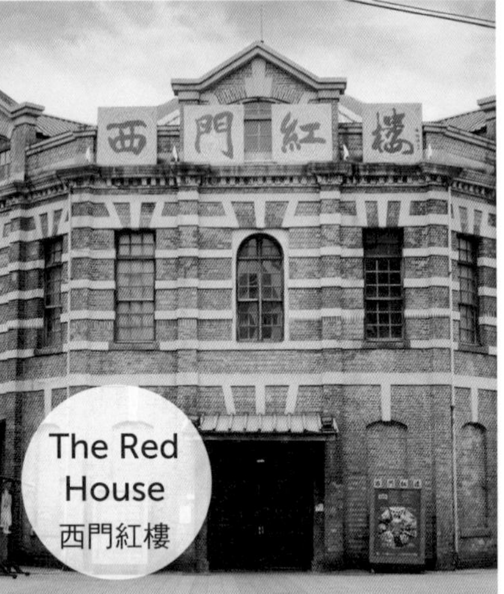

The Red House
西門紅樓

Ximending
西門町

Reading Comprehension

Choose the correct answer based on the Reading.

.... **1. What is said in the passage about people's love of shopping?** (Supporting Details)

ⓐ That it's greater than their love of food.
ⓑ That it's similar to their love of food.
ⓒ That it's not as big as their love of food.
ⓓ That it's different to their love of food.

.... **2. The main point of the final paragraph is that ....** (Main Idea)

ⓐ Shinkuchan is a great place for young people to shop and hang out.
ⓑ Many Western and Japanese fast food stores can be found in Shinkuchan.
ⓒ Shinkuchan is quite similar to the Ximending area in Taipei.
ⓓ Shinkuchan is a good place to shop for fashionable clothes.

.... **3. What is said about Jingming 1st Street?** (Supporting Details)

ⓐ It is the only shopping district with outdoor cafés.
ⓑ Most of the shops there sell European products.
ⓒ It's well known for its large department stores.
ⓓ It has an extremely fun, interesting feeling to it.

.... **4. According to the passage, where would be the best place to go and buy handmade items?** (Making Inferences)

ⓐ Xinyi District. ⓑ Ximending.
ⓒ Jingming 1st Street. ⓓ Shinkuchan.

.... **5. The author says that Ximending and Jingming 1st Street are for pedestrians only. A "pedestrian" is someone who is traveling ....** (Words in Context)

ⓐ by car ⓑ on foot ⓒ by plane ⓓ by bicycle

Dialogs

48

Discussing what to do on the weekend

Sam	Hi, Rachel. I'm going to be in Taichung this weekend and I was wondering whether you wanted to meet up.
Rachel	Yeah, that would be fun. What would you like to do?
Sam	I'm not sure really. Maybe we could do some shopping. What do you think about going to a department store?
Rachel	Hmm, I don't really want to do that, but we could go to Jingming 1st Street instead.
Sam	I've never heard of it.
Rachel	It's a really cool shopping street in the middle of the city.
Sam	What's so special about it?
Rachel	Well, a lot of people around here call it "Tea Street" because there are so many teahouses with tables out on the street.
Sam	Are there some good shops there as well?
Rachel	Yes. There are some clothes shops, a few art galleries, and places selling really interesting handicrafts.
Sam	OK. Let's go there. I'll see you on Saturday.

Jingming 1st Street

by Alvita Ko

by Alvita Ko

Vieshow Cinemas

Eslite Bookstore

49

Talking about shopping districts

Tourist	I'd really like to do some shopping while I'm in Taipei. Are there any good shopping areas in the city?
Guide	Of course. There are actually lots of fantastic shopping districts.
Tourist	I've heard about one called Ximending. Is that a good place to go?
Guide	It is. It's a really fun, exciting place. It's especially popular with younger people, and you'll find a lot of youth fashion there.
Tourist	Oh, I think I might be a bit too old for that. Where else could I go?
Guide	I would recommend the Xinyi District. There are several very good department stores in the area, and I'm sure you'll find everything you want.
Tourist	Will I find a good bookstore there? I'd like to buy a couple of novels.
Guide	There are two, actually. There's an Eslite bookstore, which is the biggest in Taiwan. It has a large section for English books. There's also a great bookstore in the 101 department store.

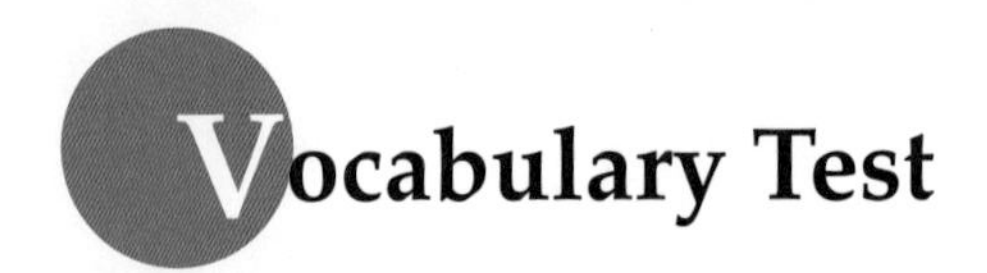

Vocabulary Test

Choose the correct word to complete each sentence.

pedestrians
dominated
agricultural
rivals
hang out
handicrafts
majestic
Consumerism
retail
accessories
luxury
gadgets

1. This department store ______________ any other in this area because you can find almost everything here.
2. Taiwan used to rely on ______________ products, but the Taiwanese economy is built around the IT industry.
3. ______________ is a social and economic order that encourages consumption.
4. Smart phones have been the most popular ______________ for Apple since the company launched its first iPhone.
5. Daan and Xinyi districts are the main ______________ areas in Taipei.
6. Ximending is ______________ by stores aimed at young people. This district is where most teenagers like to spend time with their friends.
7. The ______________ Taipei 101 was the tallest building in the world until 2010.
8. Due to the low wages they're paid, many people in this country can't afford ______________ products.
9. This area is for ______________ only. No cars or motorcycles are allowed to enter.
10. Many people in Taiwan have been promoting indigenous ______________ to foreign tourists.
11. My sister always buys all different kinds of ______________, such as necklaces, earrings, and even hats.
12. In central Taichung, Jingming 1st Street is a nice place for families to ______________.

More Facts About Taiwan

Yongkang Street 永康街

This is a small, peaceful, and calm area in the middle of one of Taipei's busiest districts. There are lots of interesting little shops selling handicrafts and traditional Chinese and Taiwanese items. If you're hungry, there's a great choice of restaurants and cafés. And when you want to take a rest, there's even a small park where children play and older people meet for dance classes.

by Alvita Ko

Tunghai Art Street 東海藝術街

Another peaceful shopping area, Tunghai Art Street is located near Taichung's Tunghai University 東海大學. As you can probably guess, there are a lot of artists and art shops along the street. Exploring all the different stores is fascinating. When you get tired, you can easily sit down and take a rest at one of the many restaurants.

The main place to go shopping in Tainan is right outside the train station. In this neighborhood, you'll find a couple of expensive department stores with international brands, rows of shops selling good Taiwanese products, and cheaper, budget outlets. So, whatever you're looking for, and however much you want to spend, you should find something in the district.

Like the Central Shopping District in Tainan, Kaohsiung's Sanduo Shopping District has stores for everyone. There are three large department stores in the area where you can find a lot of luxury products. Elsewhere in the neighborhood, you'll find smaller shops with much cheaper items. The district is also very easy to get to as it has its own MRT station.

Chapter 16 Uniquely Taiwanese Stores

Jars of Chinese medicine

Vocabulary

1 cabinet n.
2 times gone by
3 antler n.
4 fungus n.
5 aroma n.
6 produce n.
7 complex a.
8 subtle a.
9 connoisseur n.
10 bundle n.
11 lotus n.
12 stationery n.
13 carry v.
14 merchandise n.
15 toiletries n.

Reading 50

Taiwanese people don't just buy clothes, shoes, and electronic gadgets. When you walk along a shopping street, you'll definitely notice some stores that are very different from those that you see in the West. The most unusual ones are the places that sell traditional Chinese medicines. These medicine stores usually look quite old-fashioned, and they're full of old wooden cabinets[1] with drawers. You'll also see jars containing herbs, roots, and other strange-looking objects. In times gone by[2], Chinese medicine involved the use of rare animal parts like antlers[3], but many of these things are now illegal in Taiwan. Most medicines are made from plants and funguses[4], although insects are sometimes used. The people who own these stores are very knowledgeable and are able to prepare prescriptions for many illnesses.

Something else that's good for your health is Taiwanese tea. Some of the best tea in the world is grown in this country, and stores selling it can be found

Taiwanese tea

everywhere. The aromas[5] coming from these stores are incredible, and you might find it difficult not to walk inside and take a look around. You'll find shelves lined with packs of locally grown teas and tables where customers sit and sample the produce[6]. The best teas have complex[7] and subtle[8] flavors, and they can be very expensive. But unless you're a tea connoisseur[9], you might want to buy a cheaper version instead.

Another common sight along Taiwan's roads is a type of store that sells things for people worshipping in temples. They are usually very simple places, as they don't keep many items in stock. Inside and outside, you'll see piles of paper money and bundles[10] of incense and candles. Often, pieces of paper money will be folded up to make models of lotus[11] flowers.

As Taiwan has developed, some older kinds of stores have been replaced by newer, brighter outlets. Old-fashioned grocery stores used to be found everywhere around the country. With modern convenience stores becoming so popular, many of these family-owned places have closed in recent years. They still exist in countryside areas and

Tea shop

Bundles of incense sticks

Handicrafts

Flower market

on the edges of towns, though. They're usually a lot cheaper than convenience stores, and you can often find snacks, drinks, and candies that you wouldn't get in other places.

There are other interesting stores that might be familiar to foreign tourists. What makes them so special is their size. Stationery[12] stores in Taiwan are often huge places that carry[13] hundreds of different types of pens, pencils, and notebooks. You'll also find materials for handicrafts, sports equipment, gift boxes, and toys. That might seem like a wide range of products, but Taiwan's general merchandise[14] stores have much, much more.

It's incredible how many different things you can find in these places. There's furniture, tools, toiletries[15], clothes, gardening equipment, and almost anything else you can think of. Walking around a general merchandise store can be fun, as you never know what you're going to see.

↑ Old-fashioned grocery store

Reading Comprehension

Choose the correct answer based on the Reading.

_______ 1. **How are the owners of Chinese medicine stores described?** (Supporting Details)

ⓐ As being well-trained doctors.
ⓑ As being good businesspeople.
ⓒ As being educated in their job.
ⓓ As generally being old people.

_______ 2. **What is implied about temple stores?** (Making Inferences)

ⓐ They have only a few products.
ⓑ Their products are quite cheap.
ⓒ They're only found in city centers.
ⓓ They are only open in the morning.

_______ 3. **What is the main idea of the article?** (Main Idea)

ⓐ Walking into a Taiwanese tea store to look around is very tempting.
ⓑ Some stores that visitors will come across are uniquely Taiwanese.
ⓒ Most traditional grocery stores have been replaced by convenience stores.
ⓓ You never know what you'll find in a general merchandise store.

_______ 4. **"The best teas have complex and subtle flavors." The opposite of "subtle" is _______.** (Antonyms)

ⓐ fine ⓑ obvious ⓒ fresh ⓓ delicate

_______ 5. **What is said about general merchandise stores?** (Supporting Details)

ⓐ They are the biggest stores in Taiwan.
ⓑ They were a lot more popular in the past.
ⓒ They have very interesting smells inside.
ⓓ They're interesting places to walk around.

Dialogs

51

Talking about Chinese medicine stores

Jim	You really don't look well. Are you OK?
Christina	I actually feel terrible. I think I've got the flu.
Jim	Why don't you go and see a doctor? I think there's one just down the road. It'll be quick, and you'll get some medicine.
Christina	To be honest with you, I don't really like taking medicine.
Jim	OK, how about natural Chinese medicine? It's basically just herbs and plants.
Christina	Yeah, I suppose that would be OK. But does it work?
Jim	I don't know whether it will work for you, but quite a lot of my friends say it's really helpful.
Christina	So where do I get it from?
Jim	I'll take you to a Chinese medicine store. The people there will know just what to give you.
Christina	How do I take this medicine? Do I eat it?
Jim	There are some things that you can eat, but mostly, you boil it in water to make a kind of tea.

Chinese medicine stores

Chinese medicine stool

Gouqi (Chinese wolfberry)
枸杞

A Common Chinese medicine which is good for the eyes and kidney

 52

Asking about general merchandise stores

Tourist	I've seen some interesting looking stores as we've driven around Taiwan, and I was wondering what they were.
Guide	What do they look like?
Tourist	They're fairly big places and they look quite simple. They're not clean and modern like supermarkets. Outside the stores, there are usually quite a lot of things like furniture, electrical fans, motorbike helmets, and slippers.
Guide	Oh, they would be general merchandise stores. You don't really see them in the middle of Taipei, but they're pretty popular around Taiwan.
Tourist	So what can you find inside them?
Guide	That's a good question. The range of products they carry is huge, and you will often be surprised by what you find.
Tourist	So what's the difference between them and supermarkets?
Guide	Well, although some of them do have food, they mostly sell things like tools, cleaning products, and things for the home.
Tourist	It doesn't sound like a tourist shop, but I'd still like to look around one.

← Lotus flowers

Vocabulary Test

Choose the correct word to complete each sentence.

- aromas
- carry
- complex
- antlers
- stationery
- toiletries
- cabinets
- Funguses
- subtle
- merchandise
- connoisseur
- produce

1. Most wooden medicine ____________ were handcrafted and can last for a very long time.
2. In the past, it was possible to see dried sea horses, deer ____________, and even bear paws in Chinese medicine shops.
3. ____________ are not only cooking ingredients; they can also be used in Chinese medicine.
4. The ____________ from that store made it impossible not to walk inside and look around.
5. If you go to a traditional market, you will see all different kinds of agricultural ____________ from the local farmers.
6. The dish had a taste that was so ____________ the customers just couldn't get enough of it.
7. The perfume had a ____________ scent that you could only just notice.
8. He's a tea ____________, and his favorite leaves are those grown in the high mountains.
9. Most big drugstores in Taiwan ____________ medicine and cosmetics.
10. The scale of the ____________ store is amazing. There is even an elevator in it.
11. In a hypermarket, you can find almost everything from groceries to general ____________.
12. Our store provides a wide range of ____________, such as shampoo, toothpaste, shower gel, and dental floss.

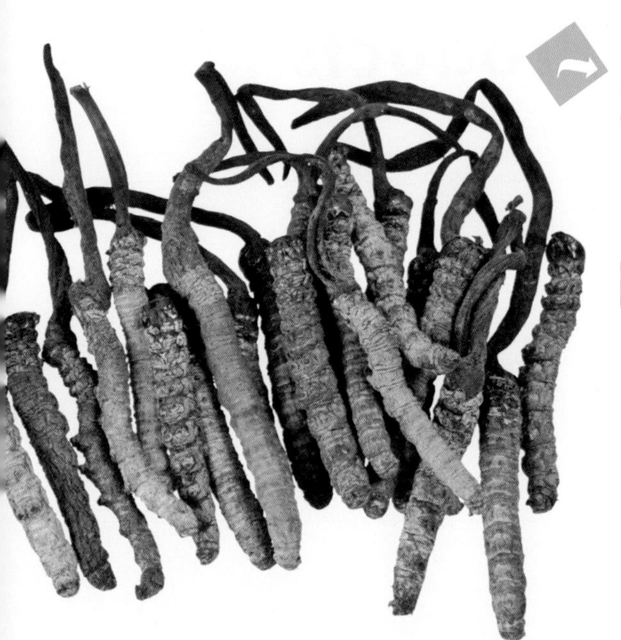

More Facts About Taiwan

The caterpillar fungus 冬蟲夏草

This is one of the more expensive things you'll find in a traditional Chinese medicine store. It's actually a kind of fungus that grows inside the body of a small insect. It is often given to people suffering from extreme tiredness. Some people also believe it can be used to treat cancer.

Marble soda 彈珠汽水

You won't see this tasty drink in many modern supermarkets, but you can find it in some old-fashioned grocery stores. The great thing about these drinks is that the bottle is closed up at the top with a marble. To open the bottle, you have to push the marble into the bottle. In the past, children used to get the marbles out of the bottles and play with them.

Chinese teapots and cups

Taiwanese tea is traditionally prepared in small teapots. It's then poured into small round cups. For some teas, connoisseurs might even use two cups. People will typically drink several cups of tea in one sitting. Because tea is so important to so many people, the teapots and teacups they use are sometimes very beautiful and expensive.

Printing stamps

Printing stamps are popular in Taiwan, and you'll see them in most stationery stores. There are usually a lot of stamps with cute pictures, cartoon characters, or phrases like "Good Luck!" on them. Also, almost everyone in Taiwan has at least one name stamp called a chop. Chops are usually bought in special stores where names are carved into wood or stone.

Chapter 17 Local Products

Vocabulary

1 souvenir n.
2 coral n.
3 miss out
4 cufflinks n.
5 jade n.
6 sculpture n.
7 fashion v.
8 cedar n.
9 supple a.
10 liquor n.
11 sorghum n.
12 alcohol n.
13 bring up
14 buttery a.

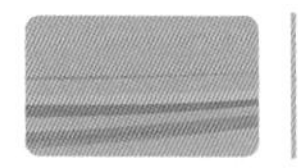

Reading

53

It's quite easy for foreign visitors to buy souvenirs[1] to remind them of their time in Taiwan. Around the country, you'll find loads of locally made products that look, taste, or feel great. One of the most beautiful things you can buy is a piece of jewelry. In Taitung 台東, bright red and pink coral[2] is used to make rings, necklaces, and earrings. And men don't need to miss out[3], as stores also sell tie pins and cufflinks[4]. The coral is harvested from the local seas and then cut and polished. As long as manufacturers don't take too much coral from the ocean, the environment won't be harmed. In Hualien 花蓮, precious green jade[5] from the nearby mountains is used to make gorgeous jewelry.

Coral and jade are also carved to produce sculptures[6]. Dragons, as well as Buddhist and Taoist figures, are common subjects for sculptors. Precious stones are also often fashioned[7] into egg shapes or pots and vases. In some parts of the country, however, you'll be more likely to see wooden sculptures. In the Alishan National Scenic Area, cedar[8] wood from the surrounding forests is used to make beautiful carvings.

Raspberry cake—An alternative to pineapple cake

Taiwan is one of the best places in the world to go if you love hot springs. You might not be able to take the water with you, but you can still buy hot spring products. Guanziling 關子嶺 in Tainan County 台南縣 is famous for its mud hot springs, and some of the local stores sell pots of this mud. It might not sound like an ideal gift, but the gray mud can be added to bath water and will leave your skin feeling soft and supple[9].

Of course, you could also buy a selection of Taiwan's special foods and beverages. Some of these have already been introduced in previous chapters, but there are many more that have not yet been mentioned. The Taiwanese do drink a lot of tea, but when they want something stronger, they might pick up a bottle of Kaoliang 高粱. This liquor[10] is made with sorghum[11], a type of grain. It's very strong and its alcohol[12] content is usually either 38% or 58%. Adults need to be careful when drinking it. This beverage is made in a few places around Taiwan, but the most famous brand comes from Kinmen 金門.

1 Mochi—A famous product from Hualien

2 Jade sculpture of Guanyin

3 Handicrafts store

↑ Wooden decorations

Tea pot

Coral necklaces

Lanterns

Kinmen Kaoliang 金門高粱酒

Gukeng coffee 古坑咖啡

Traditional Taiwanese cakes were **brought up**[13] in Chapter 14, and one of the most popular kinds is pineapple cake. These delicate, crumbly treats are originally from Taichung, but they're now made and sold all over the country. Pineapple cakes have a soft, **buttery**[14] outside and a sweet filling made from pineapple paste. As well as being the perfect souvenir from Taiwan, they're also a good idea if you need to give a gift to a Taiwanese person. The local name for pineapple, "ong lai," sounds very similar to "wealth comes" in Taiwanese, so the fruit is considered lucky here. If you don't like pineapple, There is a very similar cake that is made with winter melon.

Ong lai (pineapple) ↗

Reading Comprehension

Choose the correct answer based on the Reading.

______ **1. What can be inferred about producers of coral jewelry?** (Making Inferences)

(a) They set their prices too high for locals to afford.
(b) They're not allowed to harvest too much coral.
(c) They use fake coral in their products.
(d) They only sell their products overseas.

______ **2. Based on the passage, what do we know about the Alishan National Scenic Area?** (Supporting Details)

(a) Jade carvings are never sold there.
(b) Many sculptors live in that region.
(c) All souvenirs are made from wood.
(d) Many cedar trees grow in that area.

______ **3. Another good title for this passage would be ______.** (Subject Matter)

(a) Jewelry From the Sea
(b) Ideas for Souvenirs
(c) Hot-Spring Skincare
(d) The Lucky Pineapple

______ **4. What is TRUE about Kaoliang?** (Supporting Details)

(a) It's made in a few different places around Taiwan.
(b) It's more popular with Taiwanese people than tea.
(c) It's produced using a very special kind of fruit.
(d) It's the strongest alcoholic drink in the world.

______ **5. "Coral and jade are also carved to produce sculptures." Which of the following has the same meaning as "sculptures"?** (Synonyms/Words in Context)

(a) Songs. (b) Paintings. (c) Statues. (d) Poems.

Dialogs

Jade necklace

 54

Discussing different kinds of jade

Hazel	I think I'm going to get my mother something made from jade for Christmas.
James	Good idea. Jade is a beautiful stone. What do you think you will buy?
Hazel	I'm not sure. I'll probably get either a bracelet or a hair pin.
James	I think your mom will be very happy. What kind of jade are you thinking about getting?
Hazel	I didn't realize that there were different kinds. I thought it was all green.
James	No, jade actually comes in lots of different colors. The most valuable is bright green, but you can also get it in some other colors.
Hazel	Like what?
James	Chinese emperors often used a pale green kind of jade, and there are also brown, pink, and orange jades.
Hazel	That's interesting. I don't know what I'll get. I think I'll just buy whatever looks best.
James	OK. I'll come shopping with you if you want.
Hazel	That would be good, thanks.

Wooden sculpture of thousand-hand and thousand-eye Guanyin ↘

55

Asking about cedar wood products

Henry	What's that strange smell?
Tiffany	Do you mean the stinky tofu?
Henry	No, there's another smell—something much nicer than stinky tofu.
Tiffany	It might be the smell of cedar wood. There's a store over there selling sculptures and carvings made from cedar.
Henry	Let's go inside. I might want to buy something.
Tiffany	OK, but some of this stuff is very expensive.
Henry	Wow, these sculptures are amazing. A lot of them are of this woman. Who is she?
Tiffany	That's Guanyin. She's the Buddhist goddess of mercy.
Henry	This one is beautiful. I wonder how much it costs.
Tiffany	The price tag is on the bottom. It costs NT$6,000.
Henry	That's a lot. I need to find something cheaper.
Tiffany	How about those small, wooden pots over there?
Henry	OK, as long as they still have that wonderful smell I'll buy one.
Tiffany	This one is only NT$700 and it looks great.
Henry	It smells good, too. I'll take it.

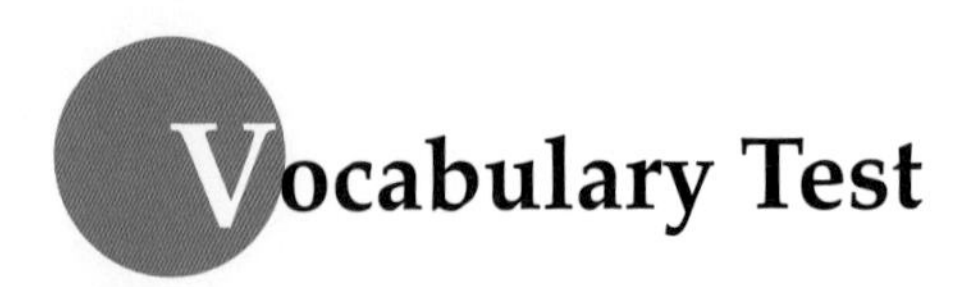

Vocabulary Test

Match the words to the correct definitions.

.... 1.	**alcohol**	.... 7.	**liquor**
.... 2.	**miss out**	.... 8.	**brought up**
.... 3.	**souvenir**	.... 9.	**cuff links**
.... 4.	**coral**	.... 10.	**fashioned**
.... 5.	**supple**	.... 11.	**jade**
.... 6.	**cedar**	.... 12.	**sculptures**

- a a certain kind of wood or tree
- b a precious stone
- c things that fasten shirt sleeves together
- d introduced
- e made
- f something that reminds you of something else
- g not hard
- h a liquid that can change the way your brain works
- i a material that grows in the sea
- j artistic objects
- k a strong wine
- l not get something

Wooden carving ↗

More Facts About Taiwan

Chiayi cubic pastry

嘉義方塊酥

In Chiayi County 嘉義縣, the local specialty is cubic pastry, also sometimes called "square cake." It's made by putting many layers of pastry on top of one another, and then sesame seeds are scattered over the top. Although they're simple, cubic pastries are very popular around Taiwan, and they're even sold as far away as Australia and the U.S.

Indigenous handicrafts

If you travel to any of Taiwan's indigenous areas, you'll find shops selling a variety of handicrafts. Bracelets are made with patterned beads and can be worn by both men and women. Different patterns on the beads mean different things, so you can easily choose the perfect piece of jewelry to suit your personality. There are also traditional paintings and colorful pieces of clothing like robes and sweaters.

Fruit wines

In the mountainous regions of central Taiwan, wine is produced using the local fruits. Plum wine is especially popular, and it has an interesting mix of sweet and sour flavors. The alcohol content of these wines varies greatly, and some are very strong, so make sure to check before you drink.

Fish candy 鮪魚糖

To most Westerners, "fish" and "candy" are two words that should never be placed together, but in Taiwan fish candy is a fairly popular snack. They're soft and chewy and taste a bit like sweet dried fish. It's an unusual flavor, and one that you'll probably either love or hate.

Chapter 18

Historic Shopping Streets

Dihua Street 迪化街

Vocabulary

1. renovate v.
2. architecture n.
3. customary a.
4. put up with
5. specialize v.
6. surrounding a.
7. picturesque a.
8. merchant n.
9. wares n. (pl.)
10. capital n.
11. baroque a.
12. arch n.
13. elaborate v.
14. facade n.
15. run-of-the-mill a.

Reading 56

Learning about Taiwan's recent history is easy. You don't have to visit museums or even read history books. For a basic introduction to the subject, all you really need to do is go shopping. That's because some of the most famous shopping streets around Taiwan were developed during the Japanese colonial period or by Chinese settlers in the 19th century.

Much of Taipei's Dihua Street 迪化街 was built by Chinese businessmen in the 1850s. Some buildings have been renovated[1] since then, but you can still see examples of traditional Chinese Fujian 福建 architecture[2] along the street. And on Dihua Street, it's not just the buildings that are old fashioned. Many of the shops sell traditional items like medicinal herbs, incense, and bamboo products. The street is especially popular during Chinese New Year, when many vendors sell customary[3] decorations and foods. If you can put up with[4] the crowds, you will find that the street is very beautiful at this time of year.

Snake Alley, also known as Huaxi Street 華西街, is in the heart of Taipei's oldest district, Wanhua 萬華. As you might guess from its name, it's famous for a particular kind of animal. Many vendors along this street keep snakes in cages, and they'll happily cook them for you. Snake meat is often served in a tasty soup, and if you're thirsty, you can try some snake blood. Other food stalls along the street specialize[5] in turtle soup.

For many years, Jiufen 九份 was a tiny settlement, but that all changed in the 1890s when gold was discovered in the surrounding[6] area. Hundreds of people moved to this picturesque[7] hillside town, and it was heavily developed by the Japanese. Many of the buildings they constructed still stand, and others have been renovated in a traditional Chinese style. The town's main shopping street is full of shops selling old-fashioned snacks, toys, and handicrafts.

Lukang 鹿港 in Changhua County 彰化縣 was once the second biggest city in Taiwan, and it had a very important port. As a result, many rich merchants[8] built houses there, and some of these buildings can still be seen in the town. Some of Lukang's old houses have been turned into cafés and stores, and traditional wares[9] are very popular here. Shoppers will see numerous stores selling Chinese-style shirts and blouses. There are even craftsmen who make

Jiufen Old Street 九份老街

Wulai Old Street 烏來老街

and sell lanterns, wooden slippers, and old-fashioned furniture. As always in Taiwan, you'll also find lots of vendors selling tasty snacks and meals.

Since Tainan 台南 was once the capital[10] of Taiwan, you would expect it to have a few old shopping streets. One of the best preserved is Xinhua Old Street 新化老街. Many of the buildings along this street were built in the 1920s by Taiwan's Japanese rulers. The Baroque[11] style of architecture was popular in Japan at that time, so along Xinhua Street, you'll see buildings with lots of columns, arches[12], and elaborate[13] facades[14]. The shops themselves are fairly run-of-the-mill[15], but tourists still love to come here to see the beautiful architecture.

↑ ↓ Pingxi Old Street 平溪老街

Reading Comprehension

Choose the correct answer based on the Reading.

_____ **1. Which of the following sentences comes closest to expressing the passage's main idea?** (Main Idea)

- ⓐ The buildings that line Taiwan's Old Streets are often very beautiful.
- ⓑ Many famous old shopping streets were developed by the Japanese.
- ⓒ Much of Taiwan's history is preserved in its old shopping streets.
- ⓓ Many Old Streets sell traditional items such as medicinal herbs.

_____ **2. What does the phrase "run-of-the-mill" refer to in the final paragraph?** (Words in Context)

- ⓐ The shops are fairly ordinary.
- ⓑ People often race to the shops.
- ⓒ The shops all sell baked goods.
- ⓓ The shops put people off visiting the area.

_____ **3. What does the author suggest about food vendors in Taiwan?** (Making Inferences)

- ⓐ They are not often found in the Old Streets.
- ⓑ They are quite difficult to find in many places.
- ⓒ They can be found in most places in Taiwan.
- ⓓ They can most easily be found in Lukang.

_____ **4. What was Jiufen like before 1890?** (Supporting Details)

- ⓐ It hadn't been created yet.
- ⓑ It was a very small village.
- ⓒ It was a developed town.
- ⓓ It was a resort destination.

_____ **5. According to the passage, why do tourists love Xinhua Old Street?** (Supporting Details)

- ⓐ They love the old goods on sale.
- ⓑ They can get cheaper prices there.
- ⓒ They want to buy Japanese items.
- ⓓ They love to see the old buildings.

Huaxi Tourist Night Market
華西街觀光夜市

Dialogs

1 convert v.
2 theme n.

 57

Asking for information about things to do in Taipei

Tourist	Hi there. I'm hoping you can give me some information about what I can do in Taipei.
Guide	Yes, of course. You should definitely go and see some of the city's old shopping streets.
Tourist	Old shopping streets?
Guide	Yes. Taipei has some great modern department stores, but the old shopping streets have more traditional stores. They will also give you an idea of what Taiwan used to be like.
Tourist	OK. So how old are these streets?
Guide	Maybe 100 to 150 years old.
Tourist	Wow! That's pretty old. I'll definitely make time to see some of these streets. Which are the best ones in Taipei?
Guide	There are a few you can visit, but many tourists love to go to Snake Alley.
Tourist	How did it get that name?
Guide	Because there are lots of stores where you can try snake meat or even snake blood.
Tourist	OK, I'll definitely check that out.

Lukang Mazu Temple 鹿港天后宮

58

Taking a trip to Lukang

Ben	So what's this place you're taking me to today?
Wendy	It's called Lukang, and it's the perfect place to find out about Taiwan's history.
Ben	It's not a museum, is it?
Wendy	Ha ha, no. It's just a really old town where you can still see a lot of traditional buildings. There's a very important old temple there, some old houses, and some other buildings that have been **converted**[1] into stores.
Ben	We have places like that in England, but they're like **theme**[2] parks and you have to pay money to get inside.
Wendy	Oh, Lukang is very different to that. It's a real town and people still live there. It's just that a lot of the shops sell old-fashioned products.
Ben	OK, I'm looking forward to seeing what it's like. Will we be able to get any food there?
Wendy	Of course. There are loads of street vendors in Lukang.

Vocabulary Test

Choose the correct word to complete each sentence.

- architecture
- wares
- picturesque
- run-of-the-mill
- surrounding
- Baroque
- renovate
- customary
- merchant
- specializes

1. The government has made plans to ______ the whole area next year.
2. The ______ on the campus is modeled after the style of the Tang Dynasty buildings.
3. It's ______ to put up decorations for Chinese New Year.
4. The restaurant ______ in exotic cuisines, such as soft-shelled turtle soup, deep-fried frog legs, and scorpions.
5. A lot of precious gems were found in the ______ area.
6. In this ______ resort, people usually feel very relaxed.
7. A retail ______ is someone who sells different goods to customers.
8. Traditional ______ are now very popular in modern society.
9. The ______ style is known for its exaggerated and fancy details, and it influenced sculpture, painting, architecture, and music.
10. Even though most of the shops here are ______, lots of tourists still come all the time.

More Facts About Taiwan

Yingge Old Street 鶯歌老街

Yingge is an old district in New Taipei City, and it has had an important ceramics and pottery industry for hundreds of years. If you walk along Yingge Old Street, you'll see a collection of stores selling beautiful pottery items. As well as bowls, cups, and vases, there are also a lot of small sculptures. You can even try making something out of clay yourself at one of the DIY workshops.

Danshui Old Street 淡水老街

This old street is just a few minutes away from the Danshui MRT station, and it runs alongside the river. There are a few interesting handicrafts stores, but this place is famous for its food. Cafés and food stalls line the street, and there's a huge variety of snacks to try. The local favorite is a tofu dish called "Ah Gei 阿給."

↑ Ah Gei 阿給

Daxi Old Streets 大溪老街

There are several old streets in the Daxi 大溪 area of Taoyuan 桃園. They're all very close together, so you can easily see them all in one afternoon. Like Xinhua Old Street, the Daxi Old Streets are known for their Baroque architecture. There's an important temple, ancient buildings, some beautiful cafés, and a range of old-fashioned stores.

Fenqihu Old Street 奮起湖老街

Fenqihu is one of the most important stops along the Alishan Forest Railway. After the line was completed in 1912, the town became an important trading center for people living in the mountainous region. The old shopping street is still popular with tourists, and if you go, you should try the famous Fenqihu rice lunchbox. People have been eating these lunchboxes for over 60 years, and they taste delicious.

Chapter 19 Night Market Tour

Vocabulary

1 attraction n.
2 surround v.
3 barbecue v.
4 a big hit
5 cutlery n.
6 purchase v.
7 kiddie n.
8 hoop n.
9 prefer v.
10 massage n.
11 entertaining a.

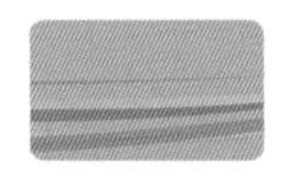

Reading  59

Night markets are among the biggest attractions[1] you'll find in any town or city around Taiwan. They are exciting places to visit because they are always full of people buying and selling lots of different things. Most people go to night markets to eat, but you'll also find stalls offering loads of other products and services. Night market vendors usually make their stalls very bright to attract people's attention. The vendors also call out to people to encourage them to visit their stalls. Apart from the noise and the lights, you will also notice the smells of different kinds of food.

The smelliest food you'll find in any night market is stinky tofu. Taiwanese people love this snack, especially after it's been deep-fried. Deep-fried stinky tofu is usually cut open, covered with a special sauce, and served with sour cabbage. As Taiwan is **surrounded**[2] by the sea, you'll find lots of seafood in night markets. Two of the most popular dishes are oyster omelets and barbecued squid. Don't worry if you don't like squid, as you can usually find someone selling **barbecued**[3] meats and vegetables as well. Western dishes and snacks are also **a big hit**[4] in night markets, and lots of stalls sell fried chicken and hot dogs.

A trip to the night market isn't just about eating. In fact, you can buy just about anything you can think of. Most things are quite cheap, so you won't need to worry about spending too much money. Some people buy all their clothes in night markets, including their underwear. There are lots of cheap items like scissors, **cutlery**[5], and alarm clocks. You'll also be able to **purchase**[6] shoes, bags, and jewelry. It really doesn't matter what you need, you'll definitely be able to find it at a night market.

Night markets are great places for families to go to as there are so many fun things to do. There are sometimes small **kiddie**[7] rides for little children to play on. And many people try to win prizes by shooting balloons with toy guns or throwing **hoops**[8] onto bottles. For people who

↑ Deep-fried fish cake (Tempura)
炸天婦羅

↓ Sugar-covered fruit on sticks
糖葫蘆

prefer[9] something a little more relaxing, there are often areas where trained professionals offer massages[10]. Finally, night markets are a good place to go to find a fortune teller. Chinese people have been trying to look into the future for thousands of years, so fortune telling is an important part of the local culture.

Some night markets are held along the city streets and others are held in special, open spaces. In smaller towns, there might only be a market once a week, but in big cities, night markets open up every evening. They are always fun and exciting places to visit. Taiwanese people love them because they are so convenient and entertaining[11], and tourists love them because they are a great example of Taiwanese life and culture.

↓ Crispy sparerib noodles 排骨酥麵

↓ Baoxin fenyuan 包心粉圓

↑ Fried Chinese buns 水煎包

↑ Thick meat soup 肉羹

↑ Hsinchu Cheng Huang Temple night market 新竹城隍廟口夜市

↓ Vendors selling Grass jelly produce

↓ Shaved ice toppings

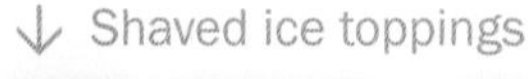

Reading Comprehension

Choose the correct answer based on the Reading.

.... **1. According to the passage, how do night market vendors attract customers?** (Supporting Details)

ⓐ They wear colorful clothes.
ⓑ They play loud pop music.
ⓒ They use nice perfumes.
ⓓ They put up bright lights.

.... **2. The author treats the subject with ....** (Clarifying Devices)

ⓐ enthusiasm ⓑ disapproval
ⓒ wonder ⓓ sarcasm

.... **3. A suitable subheading for paragraph four would be ....** (Subject Matter)

ⓐ Eating
ⓑ Everything Else
ⓒ Shopping
ⓓ Time and Place

.... **4. "Taiwanese people love [night markets] because they are so convenient and entertaining." The opposite of "entertaining" is ....** (Antonyms)

ⓐ fun ⓑ exciting
ⓒ boring ⓓ crowded

.... **5. Which of the following is described as being an important part of the local culture in Taiwan?** (Supporting Details)

ⓐ Having your future told.
ⓑ Throwing hoops onto bottles.
ⓒ Barbecuing squid.
ⓓ Buying cheap items.

Dialogs

1 container n.
2 plate n.
3 warning n.
4 reduce v.

Beef steak, noodles, and an fried egg in a night market

 60

Buying dinner in a night market

Vendor	We've got beef steak, chicken, pork steak . . .
Customer	Excuse me. Do you have any fish?
Vendor	We have squid. Will that be OK for you?
Customer	Yes, that sounds good. How much is it?
Vendor	It's NT$105 and that includes the squid, noodles, and as much corn soup and tea as you want.
Customer	Wow! That sounds great. I'm happy I came here. Where do I get the corn soup from?
Vendor	It's in that big metal container[1] over there. The bowls and spoons are right next to it.
Customer	OK. Do I pay now or after I've eaten?
Vendor	Now, please.
Customer	OK, here's NT$150.
Vendor	And here's your NT$45 change.
Customer	Thanks. Does it matter where I sit?
Vendor	No, sit anywhere you like. I'll bring over your squid in about 5 minutes. Be careful when the food comes, though. The metal plates[2] we serve the food on are very hot. So make sure you don't touch it.
Customer	OK, thanks for the warning[3].
Vendor	No problem. Enjoy your dinner.

61

Clothes shopping in a night market

Guide	We're going to the Wufenpu Market 五分埔市場. Unlike most night markets, the main attraction here is clothes, not food.
Tourist	Are there any food vendors here? I'm really hungry.
Guide	There are a few, and I'll help you find something you like.
Tourist	That's good. I was starting to get a little bit worried.
Guide	Most of the shops and stalls sell young people's clothes, but you can find things for older people, too.
Tourist	If I want to buy something, should I talk to the vendor and try to get the price **reduced**[4]?
Guide	You can do that, and it sometimes works. But you probably won't get the vendor to reduce the price by very much.
Tourist	OK, then I won't try too hard to get a better price. I actually hate bargaining every time I buy something.
Guide	Then Taiwanese night markets are perfect for you. I think you're going to enjoy shopping here tonight!
Tourist	Are things cheap here?
Guide	Yes, they're very cheap.
Tourist	Excellent! I can't wait to buy my first Taiwanese dresses. And maybe I'll get some T-shirts, too, and some shoes, and . . .

Wufenpu Market 五分埔

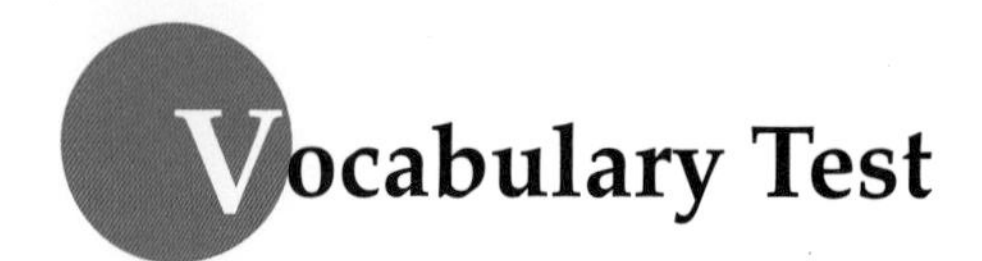

Vocabulary Test

Choose the correct word to complete each sentence.

- containers
- hoops
- a big hit
- reduced
- cutlery
- attractions
- prefer
- surrounded
- local
- kiddie
- entertaining
- purchase

1. The Eiffel Tower is one of the most famous ________ in France.
2. That country is ________ by water, so you can find lots of seafood there.
3. Taiwan has many different cooking styles, and Western dishes and snacks are also ________.
4. In Taiwanese night markets, you can easily find cheap ________, such as knives, forks, and spoons.
5. A lot of tourists love to visit the night markets in Taiwan because they are often amazed the items they can ________ there.
6. When my sister was little, she always loved the small, ________ rides at the market.
7. At a night market in Taiwan, you can often see people trying to win prizes by throwing ________ onto bottles.
8. If you ________ something relaxing, you can try getting a massage.
9. In Taiwan, seeing a fortune teller when you're unsure about something is part of the ________ culture.
10. Foreign tourists often find night markets ________ because they've never experienced anything like them.
11. You often see vendors use big mental ________ to cook corn soup.
12. Bargaining is part of the fun of shopping, so you should try your best to get the price ________.

More Facts
About Taiwan

Shilin Night Market 士林夜市

Shilin 士林 is probably Taiwan's most famous night market. It's located in northern Taipei, and it is very close to the Jiantan 劍潭 MRT Station on the red MRT line. During the busiest hours, from seven to ten p.m., thousands of people walk around the stalls looking for tasty food and cheap products.

Luodong Night Market 羅東夜市

Yilan County 宜蘭縣 is in northeast Taiwan, and its biggest night market is in Luodong. The name comes from a Taiwanese indigenous word meaning monkey. This night market is huge, and it has an amazing variety of foods and products.

Keelung Miaokou Night Market 基隆廟口夜市

Keelung's Miaokou Night Market is famous for having lots of different kinds of foods. People travel from all over Taiwan to eat there. The stalls are set out along the roads that surround an important temple, the Dianji Temple 奠濟宮. Keelung 基隆 is an important fishing port, so you can get lots of seafood at the Miaokou Night Market.

Liouhe Night Market 六合夜市

You'll find Liouhe Night Market in the southern city of Kaohsiung. As well as food and clothes, you can also buy pets in Liouhe. Don't be surprised to see dogs, cats, or even rabbits being sold here. Although it's busy, Liouhe is not dirty as students clean the streets every morning.

Feng Chia Night Market 逢甲夜市

Taichung 台中 is the biggest city in central Taiwan, and it's home to the Feng Chia Night Market. This night market grew up around Feng Chia University, so you should see lots of students there. The market is about one kilometer long. It is a good place to buy the newest cell phones at low prices.

Unit 5 Scenic Spots and Attractions

62

Shopping and eating might keep you entertained when you want to stay indoors, but to see Taiwan's biggest and most beautiful attractions, you're going to have to get outside.

The first places you might want to head to are the country's national parks and scenic areas. These beautiful locations are situated all over Taiwan, and they're great places to **get a taste of**[1] the country's amazing scenery. The national scenic areas are especially fantastic spots for tourists to come and visit. Whether they're located in a forest, coastal, or mountainous region, there will always be excellent footpaths that allow you to explore the area.

If you enjoy hiking, you could try climbing one of the country's tallest mountains. Just be aware that you need a **permit**[2] to climb some of these peaks, and make sure that you take warm and waterproof clothing. The weather can change quickly when you're at such high **altitudes**[3].

There are many ways to get around if you want to spend time outdoors, and one of the most popular activities is cycling. Cheap bikes and gorgeous roadside views mean that **pedal**[4] power should remain important in Taiwan for a long time. Of course, if you want to travel in a more relaxing way, you can board a train. In addition to the regular rail network introduced in Unit 2, there are also a few shorter **branch lines**[5] that take passengers along more scenic routes.

Those with a thirst for **thrills**[6] can try activities that will take them into the air, onto the waves, and even underwater. In Taiwan, you can try out all kinds of outdoor activities and extreme sports such as surfing, scuba diving, and paragliding.

After all that traveling and exercise, you'll probably want to go somewhere to relax, and there's no better place to do that than at a hot springs resort. Whether you **take a dip**[7] in a public pool or bathe in the privacy of your own hotel room, this is the perfect way to **soothe**[8] away aches and tiredness.

Not all of Taiwan's tourist hotspots are in the countryside, and the country is blessed with a number of historic sites. You might already know a lot about Taiwan's history and development, but visiting these places will help to **bring** the stories **to life**[9]. From temples to military bases to haunted houses, these ancient sites provide a valuable and fascinating insight into Taiwanese culture.

Finally, there is folk art and other local ceremonies. You'll see these on display at many tourist destinations, old shopping streets, and large temples. Long before TV and movies were around to entertain us all, people used to gather in villages and towns to watch Taiwanese opera and puppet shows. These traditional forms of entertainment feature music and **gripping**[10] storylines, and they're popular with people of all ages. There are also a few kinds of folk art, like paper cutting, that you might be able to try out for yourself. With so much going on, it is hard to be bored in Taiwan.

---

1 a taste of
2 permit n.
3 altitude n.
4 pedal a.
5 branch line
6 thrill n.
7 take a dip
8 soothe v.
9 bring . . . to life
10 gripping a.

Chapter 20 National Parks and Scenic Spots

Sun Moon Lake

Vocabulary

1. outstanding a.
2. boast v.
3. encompass v.
4. preservation n.
5. cape n.
6. cliff n.
7. recreation n.
8. windswept a.
9. extinct a.
10. volcano n.
11. chasm n.
12. soar v.
13. boulder n.
14. atoll n.
15. wetland n.

Reading

Taiwan is a country of outstanding[1] natural beauty. Although it's a fairly small place, it boasts[2] eight national parks and a further 13 national scenic areas. Between them, these destinations encompass[3] some of the finest scenery you'll find anywhere in the world.

The reason why some places are known as parks and others as scenic areas is that the land is managed differently. Scenic areas are set up specifically as tourist destinations, and two of the best known are the Alishan National Scenic Area 阿里山國家風景區 and the Sun Moon Lake National Scenic Area 日月潭國家風景區. National parks are still great places to visit, but the focus here is on the preservation[4] of the natural environment.

Shei-Pa National Park 雪霸國家公園

Kenting National Park 墾丁國家公園 was established in 1984. It's the oldest national park in Taiwan, and it covers the southern tip of the country. There is a wide range of landscapes in the park, but the most popular spot is probably the golden sandy beach at Nanwan 南灣. There are several other beaches in the area, and there are some amazing capes[5] where old coral has formed rough cliffs[6]. You'll also find a forest recreation[7] area, gentle hills, and windswept[8] grasslands.

Yushan National Park 玉山國家公園 is a very different kind of place. As mentioned in Chapter 1, Yushan is Taiwan's tallest mountain, and the park actually contains more than 30 mountains that stand at least 3,000 meters high. Taiwan has several other national parks in these mountainous areas. Shei-Pa National Park 雪霸國家公園 is one of them. It surrounds Snow Mountain 雪山, which is the second highest peak in the country.

Yangmingshan National Park 陽明山國家公園 is also a mountainous place. Some of the park's area lies in Taipei City, so thousands of people make their way there every weekend. Seven Star Mountain 七星山 is actually an extinct[9] volcano[10], like several other mountains in the area. As well as mountain views, you'll also find plenty of hot springs.

Within the borders of Taroko National Park 太魯閣國家公園 is Taroko Gorge 太魯閣峽谷, a huge, marble chasm[11] that runs through the park. People come from all over the world to see the beauty of this area, and it's not hard to understand why. The walls of the gorge, which are almost vertical in some places, soar[12] hundreds of meters into the air. At the bottom, huge boulders[13] litter the river bed. It's an incredible sight.

The remaining parks are all close to the sea. The Dongsha Atoll[14] National Park 東沙環礁國家公園 is hundreds of kilometers from the Taiwanese mainland. It covers Dongsha Island 東沙島 and Dongsha Atoll 東沙環礁. In addition to coral features, the area is also home to lots of marine life.

The outlying island of Kinmen 金門 also has a national park. In addition to the wetlands[15], Kinmen's traditional southern Chinese architecture and military buildings are preserved.

Back on the island of Taiwan, Taijiang National Park 台江國家公園 lies mostly in Tainan City 台南市. It contains a number of important coastal wetlands, and is home to a large variety of rare plants and birds.

Alishan National Scenic Area
阿里山國家風景區

Kenting National Park
墾丁國家公園

Taroko National Park
太魯閣國家公園

Yushan National Park
玉山國家公園

Reading Comprehension

Choose the correct answer based on the Reading.

______ **1. The main idea expressed in the passage is that ______.** (Main Idea)

ⓐ Seven Star Mountain in Yangmingshan National Park is an extinct volcano
ⓑ the almost vertical walls of Taroko Gorge are hundreds of meters tall
ⓒ Taijiang National Park contains many important coastal wetlands
ⓓ although small, Taiwan possesses incredible and diverse natural beauty

______ **2. What's the difference between national parks and national scenic areas?** (Supporting Details)

ⓐ National scenic areas are much smaller than national parks.
ⓑ National parks are not controlled by government organizations.
ⓒ National parks are more focused on environmental protection.
ⓓ National scenic areas are not as beautiful as national parks.

______ **3. As mentioned in the passage, what are some of the main attractions in Kinmen National Park?** (Supporting Details)

ⓐ Wetlands and architecture.
ⓑ Wetlands and coral.
ⓒ Mountains and volcanoes.
ⓓ Gorges and wildlife.

______ **4. The writer describes Taroko Gorge as a "huge marble chasm." A "chasm" is ______.** (Words in Context)

ⓐ an incredibly tall mountain
ⓑ a large body of water
ⓒ a type of exotic bird
ⓓ a deep crack in the ground

______ **5. What is probably the reason that Yangmingshan becomes so crowded on weekends?** (Making Inferences)

ⓐ It's Taiwan's most beautiful national park.
ⓑ Getting there from the city is very convenient.
ⓒ It's home to a rare native animal.
ⓓ In summer, its cooler there than in the city.

Dialogs

1 name after
2 long-term a.

The Calla Lily Festival 海芋季 at Zhuzihu 竹子湖 in Yangmingshan

The Flower Clock in Yangmingshan 陽明山花鐘

64

Having a walk in Yangmingshan National Park

Barry	Tell me about this place we're going to tomorrow, Yangmingshan National Park.
Naomi	Well, it's **named after**[1] a mountain located in the park.
Barry	Please don't tell me you want us to hike up there.
Naomi	No, don't worry. We are going to have a walk in a place called Zhongshan Park 中山公園. It's really nice in springtime when many of the trees are covered in blossoms.
Barry	OK, that sounds beautiful. And why did you tell me to bring my swimsuit? Are we going to a swimming pool?
Naomi	Not exactly. Yangmingshan is famous for its hot springs, and I thought we could go there after our walk.
Barry	Oh, lovely. Now I'm really looking forward to tomorrow.
Naomi	I just hope the weather is good.
Barry	What do you mean?
Naomi	The weather can change very quickly up in Yangmingshan, but I'm sure it'll be sunny tomorrow.

65

Talking about Dongsha Atoll National Park

Lisa	What are you reading?
Paul	It's a book about Taiwan. I've just read that there's a national park in Taiwan called Dongsha 東沙.
Lisa	What about it?
Paul	I've just never heard of it before. It might be fun to go there.
Lisa	Good luck with that.
Paul	What do you mean?
Lisa	Well, Dongsha isn't on the main island of Taiwan. In fact, it's about 400 kilometers southwest of Taiwan and it's not yet open to the public.
Paul	Oh, does anyone live there?
Lisa	No. There are no long-term[2] residents on the island. The only people there are researchers.
Paul	So why is it a national park?
Lisa	Because the atoll there is made from coral. It's important to preserve coral. Also, because of the coral, there are loads of species of fish and other types of marine life there.
Paul	It sounds beautiful. I wish it was possible to go there.

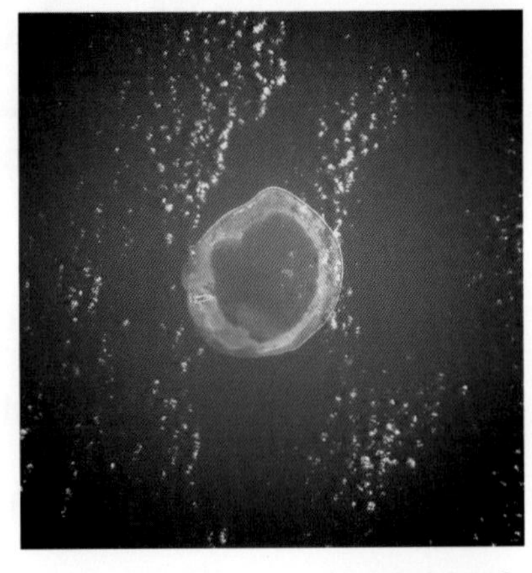

Aerial view of Dongsha Atoll National Park

Photo by NASA

Vocabulary Test

Match the words with the correct definitions.

....	**1. boulder**	....	**7. atoll**
....	**2. boasts**	....	**8. capes**
....	**3. extinct**	....	**9. chasm**
....	**4. outstanding**	....	**10. windswept**
....	**5. volcano**	....	**11. encompass**
....	**6. soar**	....	**12. gorge**

- a no longer alive
- b a huge opening in rock
- c a large rock
- d a very deep and narrow valley
- e a ring-shaped island made from coral
- f exposed to strong winds
- g include
- h has
- i rise very high
- j a mountain that has let out lava, gas, and dust
- k large pieces of land that stick out into the sea
- l very good

More Facts About Taiwan

The Northeast and Yilan Coast National Scenic Area 東北角暨宜蘭海岸國家風景區

This is one of Taiwan's many gorgeous sections of coastline. There are several great places to visit in the area. Fulong Beach 福隆海水浴場 is wide with golden sand and is one of the best beaches in Taiwan. Further east, the steep cliffs of Bitou Cape 鼻頭角 stand firm against the rough seas.

Lighthouse at Bitou Cape

The Tri-Mountain National Scenic Area 參山國家風景區

The three mountains in this area are Lion's Head Mountain 獅頭山, Lishan 梨山, and Baguashan 八卦山. In addition to having beautiful scenery, the area around Lion's Head Mountain is a great place to see some real Hakka culture. Lishan is known for its fruit trees, and the pears, apples, and peaches grown there taste delicious. On Baguashan, you'll find a giant statue of a sitting Buddha.

The Penghu National Scenic Area 澎湖國家風景區

Most of the Penghu Islands fall inside this area, so there are a lot of different things to see here. In the north, you'll find coral reefs, tropical fish, and even sea turtles. The main island of Magong 馬公 was an important trading center for hundreds of years, and you can still find a lot of ancient architecture there. In the south, many of the islands are formed from basalt columns.

The East Coast National Scenic Area 東部海岸國家風景區

This area runs from Hualien 花蓮 down to Taitung 台東 and also includes Green Island. On the mainland, most of the scenic area is squeezed into a narrow strip of land between the sea and the coastal mountains. Compared to the rest of the country, the roads here are fairly quiet, so it's very popular with cyclists.

Chapter 21

Historic Sites

Vocabulary

1 enthusiast n.
2 military a.
3 operation n.
4 reconstruct v.
5 shrine n.
6 worthy a.
7 invader n.
8 consulate n.
9 residential a.
10 controversial a.
11 commemoration n.
12 diplomat n.
13 sacrifice v.
14 behead v.
15 insight n.

Anping Fort
安平古堡

Reading

 66

History enthusiasts[1] will love Taiwan. There are lots of historic sites to see, explore, and learn about. If you are interested in finding out more about Taiwan's history, a great place to start is Tainan 台南.

To the west of the city center, you'll find Anping Fort 安平古堡. The history of this site goes back almost 400 years, as Dutch forces built a fort city here between 1624 and 1634. It was originally called Zeelandia. The Dutch used the site as a military[2], political, and economic base of operations[3] in Taiwan. As we learned in Chapter 2, the Dutch gave up control of the fort when they were defeated by Koxinga 國姓爺 in 1662.

Over the years, the site has changed a lot. The inner fort, which housed offices, a church, and living quarters, was destroyed during the Japanese colonial period. The current buildings were mainly reconstructed[4] during the 1970s, though parts of the original Dutch outer wall are still standing.

Back in the center of Tainan, one of the major attractions is the local Confucius Temple. It was first built in 1665 on the order of Zheng Jing 鄭經, the son of Koxinga. As well as being a shrine[5] to Confucius, the temple was intended as a center to train and educate worthy[6] students. Although the temple has been added to and renovated at least 30 times since it was first constructed, it still has an ancient appearance.

One of the most historic sites in and around Taipei is Fort Antonio 紅毛城 in Danshui 淡水. Spanish invaders[7] established a fort here called Fort San Domingo in 1629. They were defeated by the Dutch in 1642, and the area's new rulers built a much stronger fort, Fort Antonio, two years later. That structure still stands today. After driving the Dutch from Taiwan in 1662, the Chinese strengthened the fort . They used the site until 1868, when the British established a consulate[8] there. These latest European settlers left their mark by building a red-brick residential[9] building next to the fort. The site was only handed over to Taiwan in 1980, and it now houses a museum.

Chihkan Temple 赤崁樓 ↘

Bushido Hall 武德殿 ↓

Koxinga's Shrine 延平郡王祠

In southern Taiwan, one of the most important historical sites is Wu Feng Temple 吳鳳廟 in Chiayi County 嘉義縣. Historians believe the site dates back to 1820, although the temple was rebuilt in the mid-20th century. This is quite a controversial[10] site as it was built in commemoration[11] of a man that many people believe never existed. The story goes that Wu Feng 吳鳳 was an 18th century Chinese diplomat[12] who sacrificed[13] his life to stop indigenous groups from beheading[14] their enemies. It is now thought that Taiwan's Chinese rulers might have made up the story to convince people that they were civilized and kind leaders. Whether or not it's true, the story and controversy should give you an insight[15] into Taiwan's sometimes troubled history.

← National Concert Hall 國家音樂廳

↙ Lin Antai Historical Resident 林安泰古厝

↓ Wu Feng Temple 吳鳳廟（昔稱阿里山忠王祠）

Reading Comprehension

Choose the correct answer based on the Reading.

.... **1. Which part of the original Fort Zeelandia is still standing?** (Supporting Details)

ⓐ The inner fort.
ⓑ The outer wall.
ⓒ The living quarters.
ⓓ The church.

.... **2. The passage's main focus is on Taiwan's ....** (Subject Matter)

ⓐ Dutch invaders
ⓑ brave diplomats
ⓒ very old buildings
ⓓ wise teachers

.... **3. Fort Antonio has been controlled by several nations, but in what order did they rule the fortress?** (Sequencing)

ⓐ The Dutch, the Chinese, the English.
ⓑ The Chinese, the Dutch, the English.
ⓒ The English, the Chinese, the Dutch.
ⓓ The Chinese, the English, the Dutch.

.... **4. The author claims that history enthusiasts will enjoy Taiwan. Another word for history "enthusiasts" is history ....** (Synonyms)

ⓐ haters
ⓑ lovers
ⓒ makers
ⓓ players

.... **5. What can be inferred from the story of Wufeng about 18th century Taiwan?** (Making Inferences)

ⓐ It was a time of peace and happiness.
ⓑ The Taiwanese people were very poor.
ⓒ Taiwan was largely controlled by indigenous groups.
ⓓ The island's Chinese rulers were not trusted by the people.

Tainan Confucius Temple
台南孔廟

Anping Former Tait & Co.
安平德記洋行

Dialogs

1 confusion n.
2 complicated a.
3 fortress n.
4 consular n.
5 residence n.

 67

Planning a trip on the weekend

Beth	Where are you going this weekend?
Peter	I'm off to a city called Tainan. It's in the southern half of the country, on the West Coast.
Beth	What is there to see?
Peter	Loads of things. Tainan is a really historical city, and there are a lot of old buildings there.
Beth	That sounds like somewhere you'd be interested in. So, where will you be heading to first?
Peter	Anping Fort. This is the site where the Dutch built a fort when they arrived in the Tainan area in the early 17th century.
Beth	Anping doesn't sound like a Dutch name.
Peter	It's not. It used to be called Fort Zeelandia, but it was renamed after the Dutch were defeated in 1662.
Beth	Where else are you going?
Peter	I'm going to visit the Tainan Confucius Temple. I've heard it's a beautiful, peaceful place, and it's hundreds of years old.
Beth	I think you're going to have a great day!

68

Visiting Fort Antonio

Wes	What is this place? It's beautiful.
Anna	It's known as Fort Antonio, but sometimes people mistakenly call it Fort San Domingo.
Wes	Why is there so much confusion[1] about the name?
Anna	It is a bit complicated[2]. The Spanish built the first fortress[3] here and called it Fort San Domingo. That one got destroyed and the Dutch built this building later. However, it seems that people still like to use the original Spanish name.
Wes	OK. And what's that other building next to it?
Anna	Do you mean the red-brick building with lots of arches?
Wes	Yes.
Anna	That's the British consular[4] residence[5].
Wes	So, the British control this place now?
Anna	Ha ha, no, but they were here until 1980.
Wes	Wow, the history of this place is amazing!
Anna	I know. Let's go inside and have a better look around.

← Fort Antonio
紅毛城

Vocabulary Test

Choose the correct word to complete each sentence.

- worthy
- reconstructed
- diplomat
- enthusiasts
- sacrificed
- shrine
- invaders
- military
- controversial
- operations
- consulate
- residential

1. People who have great passion for history are often called history ______________.
2. A ______________ bunker is not a place you can visit easily.
3. When the Dutch ruled Taiwan, the island was used as a political and economic base of ______________.
4. A lot of historical buildings in Taiwan have been ______________.
5. The Confucius temple in Tainan is the oldest ______________ for Confucius in Taiwan.
6. The student worked hard and was ______________ of his award.
7. Fort Antonio in Danshui was established by the Dutch in 1644 after they defeated the Spanish ______________.
8. The first British ______________ in Taiwan was built more than a hundred years ago.
9. A ______________ building is a structure for people to live in.
10. The story of Wu Feng is ______________, because some people say he never existed.
11. To be a successful ______________, you need to be articulate and good at getting people to listen to you.
12. It is said that Wu Feng ______________ his life to stop indigenous people from beheading their enemies.

More Facts About Taiwan

● Qihou Lighthouse
旗後燈塔

The first lighthouse over Kaohsiung Harbor was built in 1863. The Japanese rebuilt it in 1916 to ensure that merchant and military ships entering the harbor would be safe. The structure was renovated in 1918, but its appearance has hardly changed since then. The lighting has been upgraded, however, and the lighthouse continues to brighten Kaohsiung Harbor.

● Taichung Train Station
台中車站

The train station was built by the Japanese in 1917, and its architecture is a mix of traditional Japanese and late Renaissance themes. Its beauty reflects the importance of the station in Taiwan's transport network. The structure was saved by a group of Taichung residents in the 1990s, and it's now listed as a national monument.

● Minxiong's Haunted House
民雄鬼屋

In 1928, a three-story Spanish-style mansion was constructed in Minxiong 民雄, Chiayi County 嘉義縣. It was built for the family of a local merchant named Liu Rong-yu 劉溶裕. Many people think it is haunted, since, according to one story, a maid drowned herself in a well next to the house. The mansion has been abandoned for many years, but it's still quite a beautiful place to visit—as long as you don't scare easily.

● The British Consulate at Takao
打狗英國理事館

Constructed in 1865, this was Taiwan's first Western-style building. To take advantage of Kaohsiung's harbor, the British established a base in the city in the mid-19th century. Back then, Kaohsiung was known as Takao 打狗. Like the British Consular Residence in Danshui, the building was constructed using a number of arches. It's a beautiful place with views of the sea.

Chapter 22

Hot Springs and Railroads

Hot Springs in Yangmingshan

Vocabulary

1. resort n.
2. mineral a.
3. sulfur n.
4. gout n.
5. arthritis n.
6. rheumatism n.
7. condition n.
8. towering a.
9. release v.
10. methane n.
11. steep a.
12. gradient n.
13. switchback n.
14. academy n.
15. kiln n.

Reading 69

Taiwan is an incredibly beautiful country, and two of the best ways to enjoy its beauty are to go to a hot springs resort[1] and to travel along one of the nation's rural train lines.

Taiwan is one of the best places in the world to enjoy hot springs, as there are so many locations around the country with naturally heated mineral[2] water. In the north of Taipei, Xinbeitou 新北投 was developed as a hot springs resort as long ago as 1896, and since then it has only grown in popularity. There are three kinds of hot springs in Xinbeitou: blue sulfur[3], white sulfur, and iron sulfur. Blue sulfur springs are good for people with skin diseases, muscle aches, or gout[4]. People with arthritis[5] are recommended to bathe in white sulfur hot springs. Iron sulfur springs are especially helpful for those with rheumatism[6] or nerve conditions[7].

Just to the south of Taipei is Wulai 烏來, another popular hot springs resort. The town is situated in a beautiful area, as it's surrounded by **towering**[8] green hills. The local indigenous people discovered Wulai's hot springs over 300 years ago, and the indigenous culture is still very important in this area. The waters here do not have any color or scent, but they are good for you and a bath will leave your skin feeling very soft.

Down in southern Taiwan, Guanziling 關子嶺 has some of the rarest hot spring water in the world. The town's mud hot springs are wonderful for the skin, and so many people love bathing there. The town is also famous for its Water and Fire Cave 水火同源, where fire actually rises out of a pool of water. The reason for this is that the stone walls at some of the town's springs **release**[9] **methane**[10] into the air, so once it was lit up, it'll never go out. Therefore, the fire has actually been burning for centuries. Along with the water coming out from the bottom of the walls it forms the amazing sight.

When you've finished soaking in Taiwan's hot tubs, you might want to take a ride on one of the countryside railroads. The most famous one of them all is the Alishan Forest Railway. It was built by the Japanese in the early 20th century to bring timber down from the mountains. Since then, it has become a major tourist attraction, as people love to see the red engines working their way up into the mountains. As well as looking fantastic, the railroad is also fascinating. In order for the trains to make it up the steep[11] gradients[12], the tracks feature a number of switchbacks[13].

Another beautiful railroad is the Jiji Branch Line 集集支線. It runs from Ershui 二水 in Changhua County 彰化縣 through to Checheng 車埕 in Nantou County 南投縣. The mountainous scenery along the way is beautiful, but the real attraction is Jiji itself. Going there feels a little like taking a step back in time. There are several historical buildings, including a Qing Dynasty 清朝 academy[14], early ceramic kilns[15], and the train station, which is one of the best preserved wooden stations in the country.

↑ Hot Spring Valley in Beitou 北投地熱谷

The mud hot springs in Guanziling 關子嶺泥漿溫泉 ↗

Water and Fire Cave in Guanziling 關子嶺水火同源 →

Reading Comprehension

Choose the correct answer based on the Reading.

_______ **1. What can be inferred from the passage about the hot-spring water at Guanziling?** (Making Inferences)

ⓐ It has a bright color. ⓑ It smells sweet.
ⓒ It is drinkable. ⓓ It is highly sought after.

_______ **2. What health condition is bathing in white sulfur hot springs supposed to be good for?** (Supporting Details)

ⓐ Rheumatism. ⓑ Arthritis.
ⓒ Muscle aches. ⓓ Gout.

_______ **3. Which of the following sentences best expresses the main idea of the final paragraph?** (Main Idea)

ⓐ The mountainous scenery along the way to Jiji is very beautiful.
ⓑ The scenery on the way may be beautiful, but the real attraction is Jiji itself.
ⓒ Jiji is home to several historical buildings, including a Qing Dynasty academy.
ⓓ The Jiji Branch Line runs between Changhua and Nantou Counties.

_______ **4. What was the Alishan Forest Railway first built for?** (Supporting Details)

ⓐ Carrying supplies up into the mountains.
ⓑ Improving the region's tourism industry.
ⓒ Bringing things down the mountainside.
ⓓ Helping mountain villagers get to the cities.

_______ **5. "The stone walls at some of the town's springs release methane into the air." "Methane" is a kind of _______.** (Words in Context)

ⓐ gas ⓑ vegetable
ⓒ building ⓓ precious stone

Dialogs

1 inland adv.
2 muscle n.
3 count . . . in

70

Planning a trip on the Jiji Branch Line

Steve	What are you up to this weekend?
Ella	I'm going to take a trip on the Jiji Branch Line.
Steve	Oh . . . are you a railway enthusiast, then?
Ella	No, not at all. It's just that this is a really beautiful railway line. It's not on Taiwan's main railway route. It's just a line that goes **inland**[1] into Nantou County.
Steve	OK, I've heard that that's a beautiful area.
Ella	That's right. Hundreds of tourists travel on the Jiji line every weekend.
Steve	So I'm guessing you'll finish your day in Jiji, right?
Ella	Actually no. I went there a few months ago, so I thought I'd go to Checheng this weekend. That's the town right at the end of the line.
Steve	What is there to see there?
Ella	I don't know too much about the town, but I've heard that there's a museum of local history and some old-fashioned wooden buildings there. It could be fun to look around.

cc by Hayato Chiou

↑ Train tickets

← Jiji station

71

Enjoying hot springs

Jim	I'm going to a hot springs resort tomorrow. Do you want to come with me?
Lindsey	I'm not sure. I've never really understood the appeal of bathing in hot springs.
Jim	What do you mean?
Lindsey	Well, it's just hot water, isn't it? I could just take a hot bath at home.
Jim	No, it's completely different. Hot spring water contains lots of minerals that are really good for you.
Lindsey	Really? What can it do for you?
Jim	Most of the water is good for your skin, and after taking a bath in a hot spring, you'll find that it's much softer.
Lindsey	OK.
Jim	Hot springs will also leave you feeling more relaxed, and if your **muscles**[2] are tired, the waters will soothe them.
Lindsey	That sounds pretty good, actually. Maybe I should come with you.
Jim	Excellent. I'm going to Wulai—it's a little town just outside Taipei.
Lindsey	OK, **count** me **in**[3].

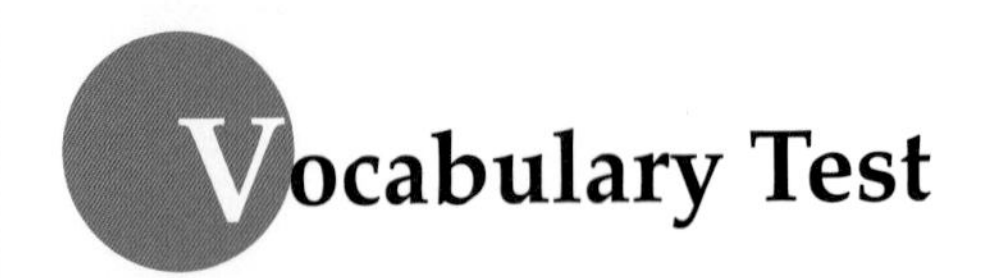

Vocabulary Test

Match the words to the correct definitions.

_____ 1. **rheumatism**
_____ 2. **kilns**
_____ 3. **switchbacks**
_____ 4. **arthritis**
_____ 5. **conditions**
_____ 6. **resorts**
_____ 7. **methane**
_____ 8. **gradients**
_____ 9. **sulfur**
_____ 10. **gout**
_____ 11. **mineral**
_____ 12. **towering**

a. ovens for baking pottery
b. slopes
c. illnesses or problems
d. vacation places
e. very tall
f. a name for painful problems that affect joints and other body parts
g. a gas that burns easily
h. a strong-smelling chemical
i. repeated attacks of arthritis
j. a problem that makes joints swell
k. a route that quickly leads from one direction to another
l. a solid chemical material

Jingtong Station
菁桐車站
the terminal station of the Pingxi Line 平溪線

More Facts About Taiwan

Shamao Mountain hot springs

紗帽山溫泉

This is another great place to take a hot springs bath in northern Taiwan. The waters here range in temperature from about 55 to 80 degrees Celsius, and they are supposed to be very good for the skin and for people with arthritis. There's a lot of sulfur in the springs here, so the water usually has quite a strong smell.

The Pingxi Line

平溪線

This is one of northern Taiwan's most popular railway routes. The area around Pingxi 平溪 used to be an important mining region, but it is now a tourist destination. People go there to hike and to see the beautiful scenery. In the future, the old mines might even be opened up to tourists.

Suao cold springs

蘇澳冷泉

Not all of Taiwan's springs are hot, and the waters in Suao's 蘇澳 cold springs measure less than 22 degrees Celsius. If you take a bath here, you won't feel the cold for long, as your body will naturally adjust to the temperature in a few minutes. Another special feature of these springs is that the water contains bubbles.

The Neiwan Line

內灣線

Like Pingxi, Neiwan 內灣 was an old mining town. Trains leave from Hsinchu City 新竹市 and head into the countryside. It's not quite as scenic as Pingxi, but the town itself is very interesting. The best place to visit is the old Japanese movie theater, which is very close to the train station. Although it has been converted into a restaurant, the movie screen is still there and old Taiwanese films are shown while you eat.

Chapter 23 Folk Arts and Practices

Vocabulary

1	bless v.	9	integral a.
2	fusion n.	10	officially adv.
3	props n.	11	point n.
4	instrument n.	12	procession n.
5	cymbal n.	13	ritual n.
6	hollow a.	14	participant n.
7	comeback n.		
8	conduct v.		

Taiwanese puppet show

Reading 72

Taiwan is blessed[1] with a rich variety of folk arts and practices that range from folk opera to puppet theater and indigenous and Chinese ceremonies. There are also a number of different activities, including paper cutting and the spinning of "tuoluo 陀螺," or tops. Many of the folk arts are still regularly practiced, and some can be seen on the streets at tourist destinations or during festivals. Although travelers might not know much about Taiwanese folk arts when they first arrive in the country, they're unlikely to leave without seeing at least one of these art forms in practice.

Taiwanese opera

Cymbals →

Taiwanese opera is believed to have originated in the northeastern area of Yilan in the early 20th century. It developed through a fusion[2] of Chinese opera with old Taiwanese folk songs and stories. Because performances are given in the Taiwanese language, the art form quickly became popular throughout the island. Although costumes and props[3] are important, the main focus of Taiwanese opera is the beautiful singing. Many different kinds of instruments[4] are used to create the music, with Chinese string instruments, cymbals[5], and hollow[6] wooden blocks featured in most performances. Taiwanese opera was once a major part of everyday life for people in rural areas, but its popularity began to fade as Taiwan developed into an industrial nation. The art is making a comeback[7], however, and should live on long into the future.

Another Taiwanese folk art that is enjoying a rise in popularity is puppet theater. Regular TV shows attract youthful audiences, and puppet theater groups can often be seen performing at temple festivals. The history of this art form stretches back hundreds of years. In ancient, rural Taiwan, companies of performers would travel the countryside and put on performances in the villages they passed through. Like Taiwanese opera, shows are conducted[8] in Taiwanese, and the language is an integral[9] part of the art's popularity.

← Puppet theater

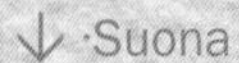

↓ Suona

The characters often use poetry and idioms when they speak.

Taiwan has 14 officially[10] recognized indigenous tribes, and they all have their own customs and ceremonies. Different ceremonies are held to celebrate stages of life, mark times of the year, and seek good fortune. During the Bunun Tribe's Ear-shooting Festival, the ears of hunted animals are attached to a pole. Men then try to shoot the ears with bows and arrows. Fathers and older brothers also help young boys to shoot the ears, believing that this will make them better hunters. The Puyuma Tribe's Monkey Ceremony ("Vasivas" in the local indigenous language) centers on hunting, and it marks the point[11] at which boys become men.

Other ceremonies are more Chinese in character, and one of the best examples is the Confucius Ceremony. This ceremony is held on September 28th each year, marking the birthday of the Chinese world's most important teacher. The ceremony, which is very serious, is held at around sunrise, and it involves a series of processions[12] and rituals[13]. Many of the participants[14] dress in traditional Chinese robes, so it should be an interesting event for tourists.

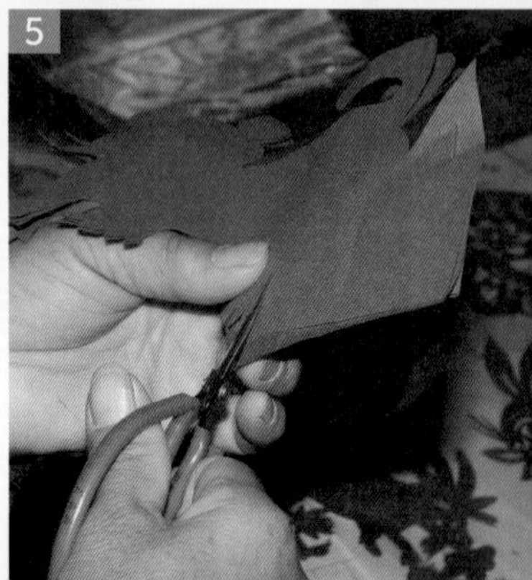

1 Dragon dancing
2 The Ear-Shooting Festival of the Bunun Tribe
3 Teenagers spinning tops
4 An indigenous ritual
5 Paper cutting

Reading Comprehension

Choose the correct answer based on the Reading.

______ 1. **Which of the following comes closest to expressing the passage's main idea?** (Main Idea)

ⓐ The annual Confucius Ceremony is an interesting event for tourists.

ⓑ Traditional arts and ceremonies are still practiced widely in Taiwan.

ⓒ Taiwanese opera has been making a comeback in recent years.

ⓓ Puppet theater is shown regularly on TV and attracts a wide audience.

______ 2. **According to the passage, what's the most important aspect of Taiwanese opera?** (Supporting Details)

ⓐ The musical instruments. ⓑ The costumes.

ⓒ The props. ⓓ The singing.

______ 3. **Which of the following can be inferred about Taiwanese puppet theater?** (Making Inferences)

ⓐ It's more popular now than it once was.

ⓑ It's more popular with the young than with the old.

ⓒ The costumes, props, and puppets are all hand made.

ⓓ The audience for puppet theater is mainly male.

______ 4. **What is the significance of the Monkey Ceremony?** (Supporting Details)

ⓐ It is the time when people can marry.

ⓑ It marks the last day of summertime.

ⓒ It marks the first day of a boy's training.

ⓓ It is the time when boys become men.

______ 5. **"[Puppet shows] are conducted in Taiwanese, and the language is an integral part of the art's popularity." A synonym for "integral" is ______.** (Synonyms)

ⓐ curious ⓑ unimportant ⓒ essential ⓓ useless

Dialogs

1 hurl v.
2 destination n.
3 adapt v.
4 intricate a.
5 lifelike a.

73

Chatting about folk arts

Laura	Hey, do you see that guy over there?
Jeffery	Do you mean the one with the spinning tops?
Laura	Yes, he's incredible. I can't believe he's able to **hurl**[1] that top through the air and make it land in that small circle.
Jeffery	He's pretty good, but I've seen better. I once saw someone throwing tops about three meters high and having them land on tiny little plates on top of sticks.
Laura	Wow! So is spinning tops a big activity here?
Jeffery	Yes. It's actually one of Taiwan's many folk arts, and you often see people or groups performing at traditional travel **destinations**[2].
Laura	Oh, OK. So can you spin tops like those guys?
Jeffery	Ha ha, no. It's fairly normal for people to learn how to do it when they're kids, but I was never really very good at it.
Laura	So, what folk arts are you good at?
Jeffery	Well, I'm pretty good at paper cutting. I've always been able to make interesting or beautiful designs by cutting paper.
Laura	You have to show me how to do that.

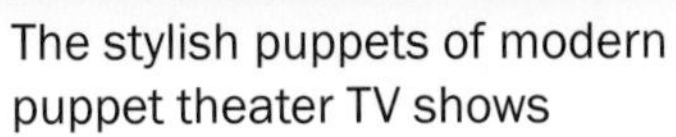

The stylish puppets of modern puppet theater TV shows

Paper cutting

74

Talking about a puppet show on TV

Jane	So, what did you think about the puppet theater TV show?
Ian	To be honest, I'm amazed. I thought it was fantastic.
Jane	I told you you'd like it.
Ian	I know, but I didn't believe you. The puppet shows we have in England are not very entertaining. They were popular about 200 years ago, but nobody watches them now.
Jane	Taiwanese puppet theater has a very long history too, but the art has adapted[3] over time. I guess that's why it's still popular.
Ian	You might be right. This puppet show used lots of special effects that didn't look old-fashioned at all.
Jane	And the puppets are quite intricate[4], so they appear quite lifelike[5] when you see them.
Ian	Yeah, but the best part was the story. English puppet shows use silly stories, so it was great to see the performance tell a serious story with lots of action in it.
Jane	That's great. I'm really glad you liked it!

Vocabulary Test

Match the words to the correct definitions.

.... 1.	conducted	.... 7.	participant
.... 2.	blessed	.... 8.	officially
.... 3.	fusion	.... 9.	indigenous
.... 4.	rituals	.... 10.	hollow
.... 5.	props	.... 11.	integral
.... 6.	processions	.... 12.	point

a. objects used in plays, movies, TV shows, etc.
b. empty on the inside
c. to take place
d. a group of people walking in the same direction
e. a combination
f. to be lucky to have something
g. pertaining to the original people that inhabited a place
h. a religious or traditional procedure
i. a person who takes part in something
j. important
k. particular time
l. agreed upon by those in power

More Facts About Taiwan

The Flying Fish Festival

飛魚祭

One of the most important events for the Tao Tribe 達悟族 (also known as the Yami 雅美族) is the Flying Fish Festival. Every year, between January and June, flying fish swim past the Tao's territory on Orchid Island 蘭嶼. The four-month-long Flying Fish Festival is held each year and begins near the start of the year. The festival is comprised of several different elements, including the blessing of fishing boats.

The Dwarf Spirit Ceremony (Pas-tai'ai)

矮靈祭

The Saisiyat Tribe 賽夏族 holds a festival to honor the spirits of a legendary tribe of short people. Legend has it that the tribe was almost wiped out by a Saisiyat man. The two remaining members of the tribe promised not to curse the Saisiyat as long as they agreed to perform certain songs and dances. The Saisiyat celebrate the Dwarf Spirit Ceremony every two years, with a bigger ceremony every 10th year.

The Amis Harvest Festival

阿美族豐年祭

The Amis Tribe 阿美族 of eastern Taiwan celebrates its important Harvest Festival in July and August each year. The festival is filled with beautiful songs and members of the tribe dress in colorful clothing. Tourists usually love to visit Amis areas during this time because the festival is exciting and it is possible for them to join in some of the festivities.

The Mayasvi Ceremony (Warring Ceremony)

戰祭

The Tsou Tribe 鄒族 celebrates its biggest ceremony in February each year. The Mayasvi was traditionally a ceremony to mark an important event such as a successful battle, the building of a house, or the renovation of the kuba (men's meeting hall). This ceremony takes place inside and outside the kuba. It ends with the singing of traditional songs.

The Wang Ye Boat Burning Festival

王船祭

These festivals take place once every three years, and the biggest one is held in Donggang 東港, Pingtung County 屏東縣. Tens of thousands of people visit the town for the festival, which lasts for several days. It all ends with the burning of a huge, hand-crafted boat. Many people believe the Wang Ye 王爺, or Royal Lords, have the ability to keep disease at bay.

Beehive Fireworks

蜂炮節

Every year in Yanshui 鹽水, Tainan City 台南市, the Lantern Festival is celebrated with thousands of fireworks. But, instead of being fired up into the air, the fireworks are blasted horizontally, straight into the crowds of people. Amazingly, people come from all over Taiwan to experience this celebration. They always dress in thick clothing and helmets to protect themselves from the fireworks.

Ghost Month

鬼月

The seventh month of the lunar calendar is known as Ghost Month in Taiwan. People believe that during this month, the gates of Hell are opened and the dead return to Earth. To keep the ghosts happy, people make offerings of food and drink and also burn paper money and incense. Since it is also thought that ghosts might try and take the lives of others, many people avoid dangerous activities, like swimming in lakes and rivers during this time.

↓ Food is also offered to gods in exchange for safety.

↓ Paper money

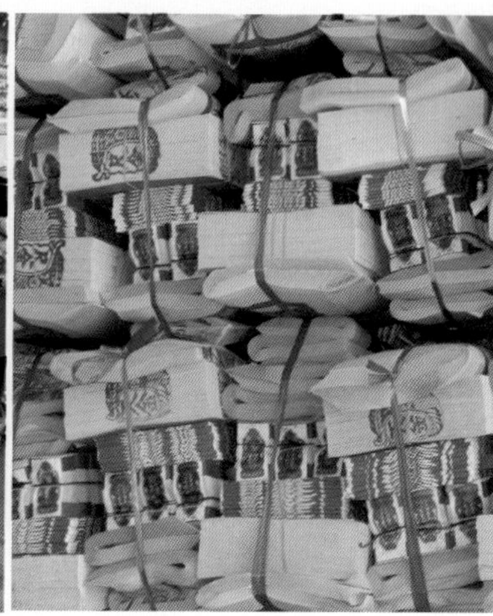

Windsurfing

Chapter 24

Outdoor Fun

Reading

75

Taiwan's good weather, mountains, and rugged[1] coastline make it the perfect country for outdoor sports. Here you'll find everything from extreme[2] sports like paragliding[3] and bungee jumping[4] to recreational[5] activities such as hiking and cycling. You can also try out a lot of water sports in Taiwan, as it's a great location for scuba[6] diving, snorkeling[7], and surfing[8].

If you've got a head for heights and love to get your adrenaline[9] pumping, then you might want to take a trip to Wanli 萬里 on the North Coast. This is one of the best places in the country to try paragliding. After being attached to a wing-shaped parachute[10], you take off from a steep hill near the sea. Strong winds quickly lift you up into the air and away from the hill. At the end of your flight, you touch down on the local beach. Don't worry if you've never done it before, as you can easily hire an instructor to take you on a tandem[11] jump.

Vocabulary

1. rugged a.
2. extreme a.
3. paragliding n.
4. bungee jumping
5. recreational a.
6. scuba n.
7. snorkeling n.
8. surfing n.
9. adrenaline n.
10. parachute n.
11. tandem a.
12. challenging a.
13. stunning a.
14. certification n.

Two scuba divers at Green Island

Taiwan is an incredible country for hikers and mountain climbers. Wherever you are in the country, you'll never be too far from some great hiking trails. If you're a fit and experienced climber, you could take on one of Taiwan's tougher climbs. Jade Mountain 玉山 is the country's highest peak, but other climbs, such as Qilai Mountain 奇萊山 in Hualien County 花蓮縣, are even more **challenging**[12]. Easier hikes can be found in the national parks and national scenic areas, and even in Taipei City, you can easily get to a good walking path. From the expensive department stores in the Xinyi District 信義區, you're only a few minutes away from Taipei's Four Beasts Mountains 四獸山.

Over the last few years, cycling has become extremely popular in Taiwan. Since some of the world's biggest bicycle manufacturers are located in Taiwan, good quality bikes can be bought relatively cheaply here. The government has helped increase interest in the activity by establishing networks of bicycle paths around the country. Riding along some of the country's more scenic roads is also a great way to see the countryside in more detail.

Main peak of Yushan

Bicycle path

When people talk about great surf spots, they generally mention Hawaii or Australia, but Taiwan actually has great waves all through the year. The best surf beaches are in the country's southeastern regions, and there's a large surfing community in Taitung County 台東縣. To find a teacher or a guide to show you the best waves, head to Donghe Township 東河鄉, which is north of Taitung City 台東市.

Another great activity that will take you under the waters off Taiwan's coast is scuba diving. This is still quite a new activity here, but there are some great locations around the country where you can dive. Kenting 墾丁, Green Island, and Penghu 澎湖, are all situated close to stunning[13] coral reefs where you can see colorful tropical fish. It's both easy and cheap to get scuba diving certification[14] in Taiwan, and once you've completed the course, you can dive anywhere in the world.

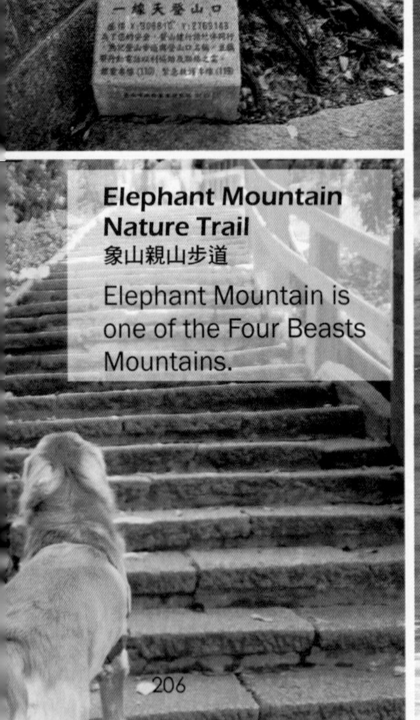

Elephant Mountain Nature Trail
象山親山步道
Elephant Mountain is one of the Four Beasts Mountains.

Wushih Harbor
烏石港
A famous surfing paradise in Taiwan

Reading Comprehension

Choose the correct answer based on the Reading.

______ **1. The passage mainly focuses on ______ activities.** (Subject Matter)

ⓐ religious ⓑ cultural
ⓒ energetic ⓓ relaxing

______ **2. Which of the following is given as a reason why Taiwan is good for outdoor sports?** (Supporting Details)

ⓐ The sandy beaches. ⓑ The good climate.
ⓒ The transport system. ⓓ The friendly people.

______ **3. According to the author, Taiwan is a good place to take part in "extreme sports." Another word for "extreme" is ______.** (Synonyms)

ⓐ risky ⓑ tame
ⓒ lame ⓓ sensible

______ **4. According to the passage, which of the following is true of surfing in Taiwan?** (Supporting Details)

ⓐ Taiwan is the best-known surfing country in the world.
ⓑ Surfers should only come here in the summer.
ⓒ Taiwan is not really famous for surfing beaches.
ⓓ The best surfing spots are in the southeast.

______ **5. Which of the following can be inferred from the passage?** (Making Inferences)

ⓐ The spring is the most popular time for scuba diving in Taiwan.
ⓑ Taiwan is a good place for scuba beginners to get qualified.
ⓒ You may see sharks while scuba diving in Taiwan.
ⓓ The best place for scuba diving in Taiwan is Kenting.

Dialogs

76

Experiencing paragliding

Irene	I can't believe you're going to try paragliding.
Andy	Why not? I think it's going to be fantastic.
Irene	Aren't you scared?
Andy	No, not really. I'm sure it's safe, and anyway, I'm too excited right now to be scared.
Irene	So how does this work? Are you going to jump by yourself?
Andy	No, I'll be doing it with a really experienced paraglider. We'll both be connected to the same parachute, and he'll be in control of everything.
Irene	So you don't have to do anything?
Andy	No. I just sit back and enjoy the ride.
Irene	I don't think I'd be able to enjoy myself up in the air.
Andy	Ha ha. OK, I think I'm going to be flying next, so I'll see you later.
Irene	Yeah, OK. I hope you have a soft landing.
Andy	Thanks. Are you sure you don't want to try it, too?
Irene	Oh yeah, I'm sure.

77

Planning a scuba diving trip

Ken	I'm organizing a scuba diving trip to Kenting next weekend. Do you want to come with us?
Mary	I don't know. I've never done it before.
Ken	That's OK. A few of my friends are complete beginners as well. You can go on a training course while you're down there.
Mary	Is it expensive?
Ken	Actually, it's not. Taiwan is one of the cheapest places in the world to learn how to scuba dive.
Mary	Are the waters near Kenting beautiful?
Ken	They're amazing. There's a beautiful coral reef there, and there are loads of bright, tropical fish.
Mary	You've convinced me. I think it will be a great trip.
Ken	Excellent. You won't regret it.
Mary	Have you been diving there before?
Ken	I have. I've been there a few times, and it's always amazing.
Mary	Great. I can't believe I'm going to scuba dive. I'm starting to feel quite excited.

Coral reefs at Green Island

Pink skunk clownfish

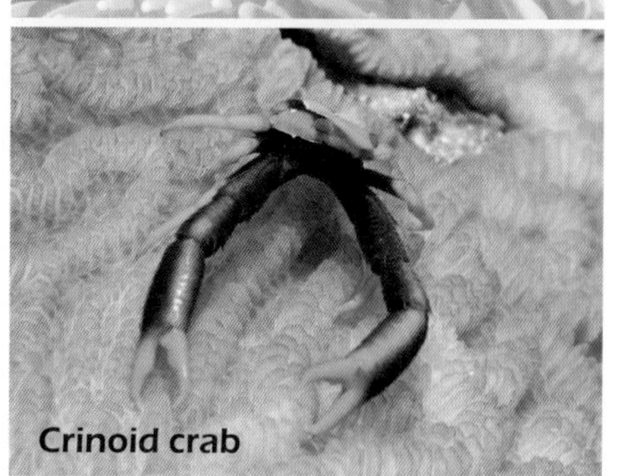

Crinoid crab

Vocabulary Test

Choose the correct word to complete each sentence.

- snorkeling
- challenging
- adrenaline
- parachute
- rugged
- certification
- extreme
- Recreational
- stunning
- tandem

1. The country's ______________ coastline has attracted lots of people who are into outdoor sports.
2. If you are a fan of ______________ sports, you can find many good activities in Taiwan, such as windsurfing, kiteboarding, and bungee jumping.
3. ______________ sports are for fun, not for rewards or money.
4. Paragliding can really get your ______________ pumping since you will take off from a steep hill and fly towards the sea.
5. You can hire an instructor to take you on a ______________ jump if you've never been paragliding before.
6. Serious climbers are always looking for more ______________ mountains to conquer.
7. The view under the water is ______________. No wonder many people love to go diving.
8. In order to get your diving ______________, you need to complete the course.
9. Double-checking your ______________ never hurts. If there's a problem with this piece of equipment, you could easily die.
10. The main appeal of ______________ is the opportunity to see underwater life without complicated equipment.

River tracing

This is a fairly new activity, and it involves following the course of a river up to its source. A day spent river tracing could involve climbing over large rocks, walking through rivers, and even climbing up waterfalls. This isn't something that you can do on your own, but you can find a few river tracing groups in Taiwan.

River rafting

There are a few places to go river rafting in Taiwan, but one of the best is the Xiuguluan River 秀姑巒溪 in Hualien County 花蓮縣. The river runs through tight gorges and moves very quickly as it goes towards the sea, making it perfect for this activity. It also means that you'll be able to enjoy some nice scenery on the way.

Marathons

In Taiwan, long distance runners have a great choice of marathons to take part in. There are marathons all over the country, and they're all in amazing locations. There are two marathons in Taipei, one in Taichung 台中, and another one that goes through Tainan's 台南 ancient streets. Then, there are three marathons in the countryside. One of them is on Kinmen Island 金門島, one is in Taitung 台東, and the last is in Taroko National Park.

Bungee jumping

There are a few places around Taiwan where you can safely plan a bungee jump. If you want to find a place near Taipei, head to Fuxing Township 復興鄉 in Taoyuan County 桃園縣. Apart from it being a safe place to jump, it's also a beautiful location, so you'll have something nice to look at when you're hanging upside down!

78

By this stage of the book, it should be clear that Taiwan has had a long and varied history. The island has been inhabited by people from across the **globe**[1] and numerous religions and languages have been introduced here. As a result, Taiwan's culture is both rich and unique, but visitors should be aware that social customs here are different from those in Western countries. If you don't want to cause **outrage**[2], then there are a few things you need to know, and a few rules you need to follow. You don't need to be careful all the time, though, and Taiwan's many festivals and holidays are usually a good time to have fun.

Unit 6

Customs and Festivals

The biggest festival of the year is Chinese New Year, and most people around the world are familiar with the event. It's an occasion when families spend time together, eat lots of food, and give gifts of money in red envelopes. This isn't the only time of year when families get together, though. Tomb Sweeping Day 清明節 and the Mid-Autumn Festival 中秋節 are also family-centered occasions, and many people will usually return home for Mother's Day and Father's Day. Most festivals are associated with special foods and activities, and each event has its own flavor and atmosphere.

Not all of Taiwan's holidays and festivals are **joyous**[3] occasions. The start of a huge **massacre**[4] is commemorated on 228 Memorial Day 228紀念日. However, most of Taiwan's special days actually have positive **connotations**[5], like when the Taiwanese celebrate **romance**[6] and love during Qixi Festival 七夕. Although this festival is sometimes known as Chinese Valentine's Day, readers shouldn't think it's simply a Chinese version of the popular Western holiday. In fact, Qixi Festival is hundreds of years older than Valentine's Day. The Double Ninth Festival 重陽節 is a time for Chinese people to pay their respect to the ancestors and the elderly.

No matter the time of year, there are a few things that you should definitely avoid doing. Public displays of **affection**[7] are not common, and they may offend a lot of people, especially the older members of Taiwanese society. Although some younger people are getting more **affectionate**[8], many husbands and wives don't even hold hands in public. While no one would **grumble**[9] if you gave your partner a quick kiss, anything more than that might get you into trouble. On a similar note, men and women in the West might greet one another with a kiss on the cheek, but that would probably cause a lot of **awkwardness**[10] and **embarrassment**[11] in Taiwan.

Another thing to watch out for is how to accept and offer things. In many situations, Taiwanese people consider it impolite to accept something the first time it's offered. If you ask someone whether they'd like some help or offer a guest a glass of wine, they might **initially**[12] say no. It's possible that they're just being polite, so you should ask them whether they're sure and also let them know that it's OK to say yes. Likewise, if somebody makes you an offer, don't say yes straightaway or they might think that you're **greedy**[13] or rude.

1 globe n.
2 outrage n.
3 joyous a.
4 massacre n.
5 connotation n.
6 romance n.
7 affection n.
8 affectionate a.
9 grumble v.
10 awkwardness n.
11 embarrassment n.
12 initially adv.
13 greedy a.

Chapter 25

Customs and Etiquette

The elderly tend to receive more respect in Taiwan than they do in the West.

Vocabulary

1 respectful a.
2 behavior n.
3 etiquette n.
4 social standing
5 sibling n.
6 fairly adv.
7 status n.
8 gap n.
9 humiliate v.
10 gender n.
11 vulgar a.
12 offensive a.
13 uncivilized a.

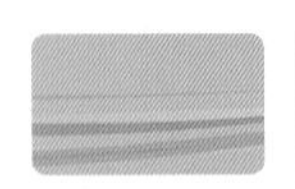

Reading 79

Being polite and respectful[1] is important in both Taiwan and the West. In both places, there are rules of behavior[2] that you should follow if you don't want to offend people. These rules sometimes appear very similar, and people from both cultures might show their respect to someone in exactly the same way. Despite this, however, the Taiwanese system of etiquette[3] is sometimes very different from the Western system. As a result, somebody from one culture might easily offend somebody from the other without ever intending to.

In Taiwanese society, there are clear rules regarding social standing[4]. Parents, older siblings[5], teachers, and bosses have a higher position and should be respected. In the West, however, the idea of social standing has lost most of its importance over the last 200 years. Nowadays, everyone is supposed to be fairly[6] respectful of everyone else. So, although bosses have a higher status[7] than employees, they're still expected to respect their workers. If they don't, they probably won't be treated very well by their employees. Older brothers and sisters don't really have a higher position in a family than their younger siblings, and elderly people actually sometimes receive less rather than more respect.

In many Taiwanese families, men have a higher standing than women, but things are changing and the gap[8] between the sexes isn't as big as it used to be. Yet even in modern Taiwan, there are still cases of men and women being treated differently by family members. During family occasions, it is usually the women who prepare and serve the food while the men sit back and relax. In the past, it was even thought that a man would be humiliating[9] himself by stepping into a kitchen. In the West, there are some families where these kinds of gender[10] differences still exist, but they are usually regarded as old fashioned.

Women usually prepare and serve food without help from their families.

In addition to all of this, there are many actions that might be perfectly acceptable in one culture but vulgar[11] or offensive[12] in another. A lot of them concern food and how it should be eaten. To a Westerner, it might seem convenient to just stick your chopsticks into your bowl of food when you're not using them, but doing this would be a mistake. A pair of chopsticks sticking up from a bowl look like sticks of incense offered to a dead ancestor, so this action would be very offensive to those at the same table. In Taiwan, many people hold their food bowls towards their mouths when eating, but this is considered uncivilized[13] in the West, where it's also unacceptable to drink soup directly from a bowl or to put your knife in your mouth.

In Taiwan, four is a very unlucky number because in Chinese, it sounds like the word for "death" or "die." As a result, some apartment buildings and almost all hospitals do not have a fourth floor. In the West, however, the number 13 is considered unlucky. One possible reason for this is that there were 13 people at Jesus Christ's last meal.

↘ Chopsticks should be put on the rim of the bowl or on the table beside the bowl instead of being stuck into the food.

Reading Comprehension

Choose the correct answer based on the Reading.

______ **1. Which of the following would the author most likely say to someone going abroad?** (Making Inferences)

ⓐ Following the local rules of etiquette is optional.
ⓑ There's no need to apologize if you accidentally offend someone.
ⓒ You should learn the local etiquette to avoid causing offense.
ⓓ Offending someone from another country is no big deal.

______ **2. Which of the following actions is acceptable in the West?** (Supporting Details)

ⓐ Licking your plate clean after eating.
ⓑ Holding your plate to your mouth.
ⓒ Drinking your soup from your bowl.
ⓓ Putting your fork into your mouth.

______ **3. According to the passage, how is etiquette different in Taiwan and the West?** (Supporting Details)

ⓐ People care less about social standing in the West.
ⓑ Social standing is much more important in the West.
ⓒ Old people usually respect young people in the West.
ⓓ Employees never respect their bosses in the West.

______ **4. "Parents, older siblings, teachers, and bosses have a higher position and should be respected." "Siblings" probably means ______.** (Words in Context)

ⓐ foreign visitors
ⓑ brothers and sisters
ⓒ actors and actresses
ⓓ gods and goddesses

______ **5. The main idea of the passage is that ______.** (Main Idea)

ⓐ certain customs and rules of etiquette are different in Taiwan than the West
ⓑ there are many differences between Taiwan and the West
ⓒ the number four is unlucky in Taiwan, while in the West it's the number 13
ⓓ old-fashioned gender roles are more common in Taiwan than in the West

Dialogs

1 devil n.
2 nibble v.

80

Talking about unlucky numbers

Maggie	Which floor does Richard live on?
Paul	I think his apartment is on the fifth floor.
Maggie	OK, I'll press the button. Hold on . . . where's the button for the fourth floor?
Paul	There isn't a fourth floor.
Maggie	What do you mean?
Paul	Well, the floors are numbered one, two, three, and then five.
Maggie	Why isn't there a fourth floor?
Paul	Because four is a very unlucky number for Taiwanese people. The Chinese word for four sounds the same as the word for death.
Maggie	So if you had an apartment on the fourth floor, it would be like you lived on the death floor?
Paul	Kind of, yeah. A lot of apartment buildings still have a fourth floor, but most hospitals don't.
Maggie	Oh, OK. In America, 13 is the unluckiest number.
Paul	I thought it was 666.
Maggie	The number 666 is considered to be the mark of the devil[1], but it is the number 13 that we think of as unlucky.

↓ Sticking chopsticks into food is considered very inappropriate in Taiwan.

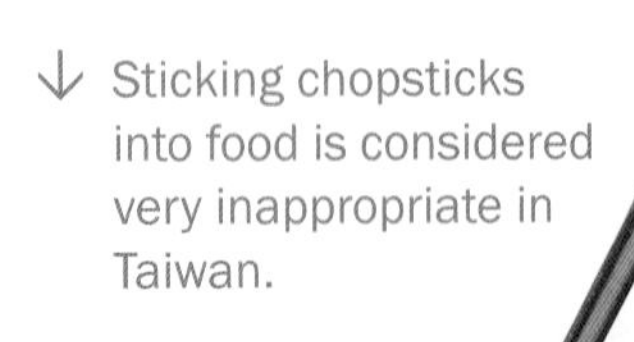

81

Discussing table manners

Joe	How was dinner with your boyfriend's family last night?
Andrea	It was interesting. That was the first time I've eaten with a Taiwanese family, and it's a bit different from America.
Joe	I guess it would be.
Andrea	One thing that surprised me was that my boyfriend and his father did nothing to help his mother and sister bring the food to the table or clear away the dishes.
Joe	In a lot of families, men don't really do that. Did you help?
Andrea	Yes. In America it would be a bit strange for a guest to help, but I felt sorry for my boyfriend's mother.
Joe	Was anything else strange?
Andrea	Yes. When I ate pieces of chicken, I **nibbled**[2] at the meat and left the fat and bones. But they would put the whole piece in their mouth, then pull out the bones and leave them on the table.
Joe	That doesn't happen in America?
Andrea	No! It looks horrible!

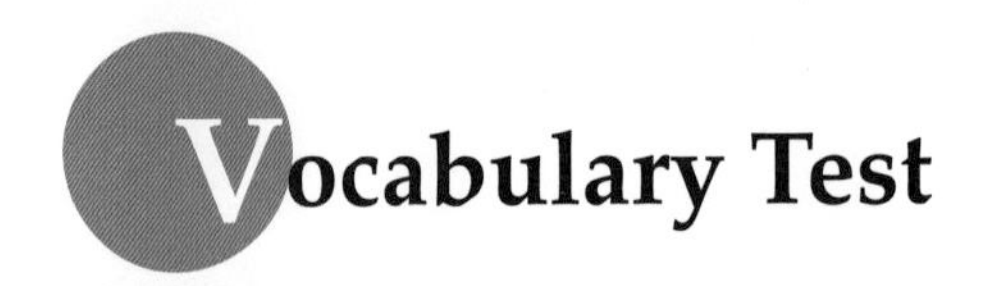

Vocabulary Test

Choose the correct word to complete each sentence.

- status
- social standing
- vulgar
- etiquette
- uncivilized
- fairly
- Gender differences
- respectful
- offensive
- gap
- humiliating
- behavior

1. If you say bad things to people, they will think you're not ....
2. In different cultures, there are different rules for ....
3. The proper .... in the West is that men would open doors for women.
4. In many Asian countries, teachers have a high ....
5. In modern society, both men and women should be treated ....
6. Her .... in the company rose after she got a promotion.
7. At the start of the year, he was a long way behind the other students, but he's worked hard to close the ....
8. In the past, it was considered .... for men to help out in the kitchen.
9. .... in the West are not as obvious as in Asia.
10. In Muslim countries, kissing a lady on the check in public is terribly ....
11. Spitting on the streets is considered unsanitary and ....
12. Talking loudly on your cell phone in a theater is really rude and ....

Gift giving

In Taiwan, you should never give people clocks as gifts. In Chinese, to give someone a clock means the same thing as sending someone on their final journey. In Taiwan, it's quite normal to give people fruit, but this would be unusual in the West. Common gifts would be chocolate, candy, and cookies.

The curse of the umbrella

In Taiwan, you should always close your umbrella before you go inside someone's home. People believe that if your umbrella is open, you might take evil spirits into a house. Funnily enough, people in the West also believe it's very bad luck to open an umbrella indoors.

Be careful where you place your bed

Traditionally, when someone died in Taiwan, their body was put in a coffin and left in the family house for a few days. The dead person was always positioned so that their feet pointed towards the door. Therefore, some people believe it's very bad luck to sleep with your feet pointing towards the bedroom door.

Bad luck in the West

In the West, there are a few actions that people believe will bring you bad luck. People say that you shouldn't walk under a ladder or step on cracks in the sidewalk. You also shouldn't spill salt or look at a new moon over your left shoulder, but the worst thing of all is to break a mirror. People say that doing this will bring you seven years of bad luck. Although some people take these things very seriously, most people think they're nonsense.

Chapter 

Holidays and Festivals (1)

 Reading  82

Chinese New Year is the biggest and most important festival of the year in Taiwan. Like Christmas in the West, it is a time for families, food, fun, and gifts. Couplets[1] about luck or wealth are posted around people's doors, and firecrackers are set off. As with most of Taiwan's festivals, Chinese New Year follows the lunar calendar, so it doesn't have a fixed date on the more commonly used solar calendar. The New Year could fall anytime between late January and late February.

The New Year festivities really begin on New Year's Eve. Most families get together for a large meal that traditionally involves a few special foods like fish and a type of greens called "long-year vegetables." People say that since the Chinese word for fish sounds the same as the word for surplus[2], you can't eat all the fish. If you do, your family won't have any extra food or money for the whole year. After eating, families usually stay up very late, and the traditional belief is that the longer you stay awake, the longer your parents will live.

Vocabulary

1 couplet n.
2 surplus n.
3 grant v.
4 legend n.
5 amuse v.
6 imaginative a.
7 tomb n.
8 cremate v.
9 remain n.
10 deceased a.

↑ Taiwanese people usually go to temples during Chinese New Year to pray for luck and wealth in the coming year.

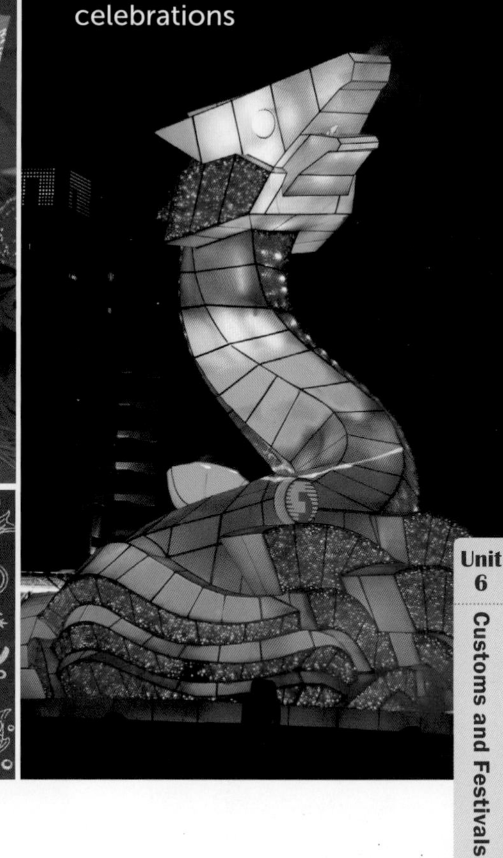

↑ Couplets

On New Year's Day, you're supposed to wear new clothes. Although some people don't follow this tradition anymore, you do still see little children wearing bright, new clothes on this day. This is also the day when red envelopes are given. When children are young, they get envelopes from other people in the family, but when they grow up and begin earning money, they need to give envelopes to their parents.

Although people are only **granted**[3] a few days off work, the festival doesn't end until the 15th day of the New Year. This day is marked by the Lantern Festival, and it's a time when bright lanterns light up the night sky. There are many different **legends**[4] about the origins of the Lantern Festival, and while some say that lanterns were first lit to **amuse**[5] fun-loving gods, others say they were used to confuse a god who wanted to destroy a village.

In modern Taiwan, parks and streets in cities around the country are decorated with hundreds of beautiful lanterns. Some of these lanterns have very **imaginative**[6] designs and others are extremely large. Not surprisingly, then, these displays usually attract thousands of visitors.

The next festival on the calendar is Tomb[7] Sweeping Day. It usually falls on April 5th, and it always comes 104 days after the shortest day of the year. Traditionally, this is the time of year when people should head out to enjoy springtime and when families should sweep and clean the tombs of their ancestors. Since Taiwan is a small, overcrowded island, people are increasingly being cremated[8] when they die. Their ashes are then placed in special buildings with room for hundreds of people's remains[9]. Since there are fewer tombs than there used to be, Tomb Sweeping Day is losing some of its importance in Taiwan. That said, many families still do spend the day clearing the weeds away from their deceased[10] relatives' tombs. After cleaning the site, they burn incense and paper money for their ancestors.

1 Firecrackers 鞭炮

2 Year cake 年糕

3 Lion dancing 舞獅

4 Melon seeds 瓜子

5 New Year supplies 年貨

6 Fish 魚

7 Reunion dinner 團圓飯

Reading Comprehension

Choose the correct answer based on the Reading.

_______ **1. Another title for the passage could be _______.** (Subject Matter)

ⓐ Cleaning Tombs
ⓑ Christmas in the East
ⓒ Annual Celebrations
ⓓ The Fish of Wealth

_______ **2. What is said in the passage about the lunar calendar?** (Supporting Details)

ⓐ It's used to work out when Taiwan's festivals are.
ⓑ It's used to work out when Western festivals are.
ⓒ It's used far more often than the solar calendar.
ⓓ It might replace the solar calendar in the future.

_______ **3. "Some of these lanterns have very imaginative designs and others are extremely large." Something that is "imaginative" is NOT _______.** (Antonyms)

ⓐ fanciful ⓑ original ⓒ creative ⓓ dull

_______ **4. According to the passage, how did Lantern Festival begin?** (Supporting Details)

ⓐ It's unclear, as there's more than one story.
ⓑ People were trying to confuse an angry god.
ⓒ Children wanted to decorate their villages.
ⓓ The lights made it safer for people at night.

_______ **5. The article suggests that the more crowded Taiwan gets in the future, _______.** (Making Inferences)

ⓐ the less people will honor their ancestors
ⓑ the less people will be buried in tombs
ⓒ the more people will want to move abroad
ⓓ the more polluted Taiwan will get

Dialogs

1 zodiac n.
2 characteristics n.
3 personality n.
4 self-centered a.
5 unpredictable a.
6 short-tempered a.
7 elegant a.
8 release v.
9 underneath prep.

83 Discussing the Chinese **zodiac**[1]

Emily	It's Chinese New Year next week, right?
James	Yes, that's right. It's going to be the Year of the Dragon.
Emily	What does that mean – the Year of the Dragon?
James	According to Chinese beliefs, each year is connected to an animal. There are twelve animals in total.
Emily	And the dragon is one of those animals?
James	Exactly. The animals have different **characteristics**[2], so people in each year are supposed to have different **personalities**[3].
Emily	So what about people born in the Year of the Dragon?
James	They're supposed to be powerful and energetic, but they can be **self-centered**[4].
Emily	What animal are you?
James	I'm a horse, so that means I should be cheerful, **unpredictable**[5], and sometimes **short-tempered**[6].
Emily	That's pretty accurate. I was born on April 22, 1987, so what animal am I?
James	That would make you a rabbit. You're supposed to be very lucky, polite, and **elegant**[7].

Pingxi Sky Lantern Festival
| 平溪天燈節

84 Going to Lantern Festival

Jack	What are you doing this weekend?
Doris	I'm visiting a friend in Kaohsiung, and I think we're going to look at the Lantern Festival displays along Love River.
Jack	You're going to look at lanterns?
Doris	Yeah, it's supposed to be really nice. It's always quite nice to walk along the river, and my friend says the lanterns are really interesting. People make them using all different designs, so some of them look like cartoon characters and others look like buildings.
Jack	I thought lanterns were always just round.
Doris	Maybe they were traditionally, but people are quite imaginative with them now.
Jack	You've got me interested. Are there any Lantern Festival displays in or around Taipei?
Doris	Yes, there's one in Taipei almost every year. You could also take a trip to Pingxi where they **release**[8] sky lanterns every year.
Jack	What are sky lanterns?
Doris	They're a bit like little hot air balloons. You light a fire **underneath**[9] them and they float away into the sky.

Vocabulary Test

Match the words to the correct definitions.

.... 1. **tomb**

.... 2. **legends**

.... 3. **cremated**

.... 4. **surplus**

.... 5. **lunar**

.... 6. **fall**

.... 7. **imaginative**

.... 8. **amuse**

.... 9. **solar**

.... 10. **granted**

.... 11. **firecracker**

.... 12. **couplet**

a given

b something that explodes with a loud bang

c relating to the moon

d entertain

e a short poem

f a place where people are buried

g an old story that might not be true

h about the sun

i creative

j happen at a particular time

k burning of a dead body

l extra things

January 1 Lunar Calendar

New Year

Often called "yuan dan" 元旦 meaning "the first day," January 1st is the first holiday of the year in Taiwan. Traditionally, it wasn't celebrated at all, and many older people will not make an effort to stay up after midnight on New Year's Eve. Young people often do meet up with their friends on December 31st and stay up late. The biggest New Year party in the country takes place outside Taipei 101, and it features an amazing fireworks display.

April 4

Children's Day

This day in honor of children is celebrated around the world, though countries have chosen their own dates for the holiday. In Taiwan, Children's Day falls on April 4th, and it coincides with Women's Day 婦女節. This is a national holiday, so schools and some businesses close for the day.

February 28

Peace Memorial Day

The 228 Incident 228事件 was a massacre of thousands of Taiwanese citizens that began on February 28th, 1947. One day earlier, citizens in Taiwan began a huge protest against the government. The government responded by brutally killing anyone connected with the protest. It is thought that between 10,000 and 30,000 people were killed. The incident is remembered with a national holiday on February 28th, which is now referred to as Peace Memorial Day 和平紀念日 or 228 Memorial Day 228紀念日.

May 1

Labor Day

On May 1st many businesses, especially those related to manufacturing, close for the day, as do banks, in Taiwan. However, many government offices and schools stay open. Although it's known as Labor Day here, it's also called May Day and International Workers' Day in other places. The day is often marked by workers holding demonstrations to demand better wages and working conditions.

Chapter 27

Holidays and Festivals (2)

Vocabulary

1	statesman n.	8	sweetheart n.
2	sb./sth. has it	9	permit v.
3	distress v.	10	desperate a.
4	spectator n.	11	appease v.
5	shell ginger n.	12	hazardous a.
6	magpie n.	13	whistle v.
7	pity n.	14	dub v.

Reading  85

On the fifth day of the fifth lunar month, the Taiwanese celebrate the Dragon Boat Festival 端午節. The event commemorates the death of Qu Yuan 屈原, a third-century statesman[1] and poet who lived in China's Chu kingdom. When Qin 秦 forces took over Chu 楚, Qu Yuan killed himself by throwing himself into a river. Legend has it[2] that the local people were so distressed[3] by this that they sailed up and down the river looking for his body. They even threw rice dumplings into the water, hoping that the fish would eat the food instead of Qu Yuan's body.

Present day celebrations are based on this story. Dragon boat races have become very popular, and teams now come to Taiwan from all over the world to take part in the events. Races are fun events and the colorfully decorated boats attract crowds of spectators[4]. Rice dumplings, or "zong zi 粽子," are commonly eaten at this time of year. There are several different kinds of dumplings, most

Dragon Boat Race

Pomelos

Offerings

of which feature sticky rice, meat, and mushrooms wrapped in bamboo or shell ginger[5] leaves.

On the seventh day of the seventh lunar month, people celebrate Qixi 七夕 Festival, which is sometimes known as Chinese Valentine's Day. Legend has it that two young lovers were sent to different stars by the goddess of Heaven. She then separated the stars by creating a river between them. The magpies[6] of the world took pity[7] on the lovers, and decided to make a bridge over the river once a year so that the sweethearts[8] could be united. Just like Western Valentine's Day, people celebrate the day by giving their partners gifts.

During the Ghost Festival 中元節, it is believed that the gates of Hell are opened and the dead are permitted[9] to return to Earth. Traditionally in China, people say this happens on the 15th day of the seventh lunar month. In Taiwan, however, many people believe ghosts are with us throughout the seventh month, and the period is therefore known as Ghost Month 鬼月.

People believe that ghosts are so desperate[10] for a new life that they might take the lives of other people. To appease[11] the ghosts, people offer food, incense, and paper money to them during Ghost Month. They also avoid hazardous[12] activities like swimming in lakes and rivers. They don't whistle[13] or talk about ghosts to avoid attracting them.

The last main festival of the year is the Mid-Autumn Festival 中秋節, and it falls on the 15th day of the eighth lunar month. The day has also been dubbed[14] Moon Festival, and the moon plays an important role in the celebrations. An old legend says that a beautiful woman named Chang E 嫦娥 lives on the moon. Once a year, on Mid-Autumn Festival, she is visited by her husband, Hou Yi 后羿, and the moon shines more brightly as a result. In Taiwan, this is a day for families to spend time together. People often barbecue outside their homes and eat moon cakes.

Zong zi (rice dumplings)

Moon cake

Sachet

Ghost Month Parade

Reading Comprehension

Choose the correct answer based on the Reading.

_____ 1. **What can be inferred from the passage about Qu Yuan, the third-century statesman?** (Making Inferences)

ⓐ He had a violent temper.
ⓑ He was a much-loved figure.
ⓒ He supported the Qin forces.
ⓓ He could not swim.

_____ 2. **Why, according to the legend, does the moon shine more brightly on Mid-Autumn Festival?** (Supporting Details)

ⓐ Because Chang E is angry on that day.
ⓑ Because Chang E is reunited with her husband on that day.
ⓒ Because Chang E has a party in the moon on that day.
ⓓ Because Chang E cleans the moon on that day.

_____ 3. **According to the legend of Qixi, who created a river between two stars?** (Supporting Details)

ⓐ The goddess of Heaven.
ⓑ A pair of young lovers.
ⓒ All the world's magpies.
ⓓ Chang E.

_____ 4. **The main idea of the first two paragraphs is that _____.** (Main Idea)

ⓐ the local people sailed up and down the river looking for Qu Yuan's body
ⓑ people race beautifully decorated boats on Dragon Boat Festival
ⓒ zong zi, special rice dumplings, are eaten on Dragon Boat Festival
ⓓ today's Dragon Boat Festival celebrations are based on the story of Qu Yuan

_____ 5. **"To appease the ghosts, people offer food, incense, and paper money to them during Ghost Month." If you "appease" someone, you _____.** (Words in Context)

ⓐ make them sad by giving them bad news
ⓑ make them angry by offending them
ⓒ make them calm by giving them what they want
ⓓ make them happy by telling them a joke

Dialogs

1 triangular a.
2 pyramid n.
3 drown v.
4 archer n.
5 immortality n.

 86

Discussing zong zi, or rice dumplings

Tom	I keep seeing these **triangular**[1] things in food shops. Do you know what they are?
Amy	Are they like little **pyramids**[2]?
Tom	Yes.
Amy	And wrapped in leaves?
Tom	Yes. What are they?
Amy	They're rice dumplings called "zong zi," and they're really popular around the time of Dragon Boat Festival.
Tom	Why?
Amy	Well, the festival started when people rowed their boats across a river looking for an important person who **drowned**[3] himself in the water.
Tom	Oh right.
Amy	They also dropped rice dumplings in the water so the fish wouldn't want to eat the person's body.
Tom	So what's inside them?
Amy	There's sticky rice and some fillings. Most shops and families use slightly different recipes, so there are lots of different kinds. My mom makes them with pork, peanuts, and dried shrimp.
Tom	Sounds tasty.
Amy	I'll bring you some if you want. My mom makes loads every year.
Tom	That would be great. Thank you.

87

Telling the story of Chang E and Hou Yi

Marie	A Taiwanese told me that people here believe there's a woman living on the moon.
Gary	That's not entirely true. There's an old story about a woman called Chang E who's supposed to live on the moon, but we don't really believe it.
Marie	So what's the story?
Gary	Well, Chang E used to live on Earth with her husband, Hou Yi, who was a brilliant **archer**[4].
Marie	So did he shoot her up to the moon?
Gary	No. The story goes that there were once 10 suns, and when they started to burn the earth, Hou Yi shot nine of them down. Hou Yi went to the Queen Mother of the West searching for **immortality**[5] and was given a pill that would allow him to live forever.
Marie	Right.
Gary	Instead of eating it, he hid it in his home.
Marie	And then Chang E ate it instead?
Gary	Exactly, and then she floated up to the moon.
Marie	Wow, that's a crazy story.

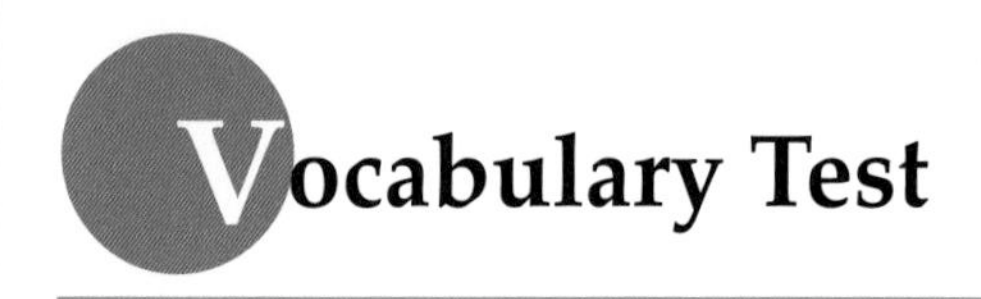

Vocabulary Test

Match the words to the correct definitions.

........1.	**hazardous**	........7.	**magpies**
........2.	**appease**	........8.	**pity**
........3.	**sth./sb. has it**	........9.	**reed**
........4.	**whistle**	........10.	**sweethearts**
........5.	**dubbed**	........11.	**distressed**
........6.	**statesman**	........12.	**spectators**

a named

b people in love

c very dangerous

d a plant that grows in or near water

e says that something is true

f worried or very sad

g keep somebody happy

h politician

i the feel of sympathy

j make a noise by blowing through your lips

k people watching something

l black and white birds

May — the second Sunday

MOTHER'S DAY

In Taiwan, people celebrate Mother's Day on the second Sunday of May every year. As in the rest of the world, it's a day for honoring and appreciating mothers. Children usually either travel home or call their mothers on this special day. As of the year 2000, the second Sunday in May has also been known as Buddha Day 佛誕節 in Taiwan, so people might also make an effort to visit a temple.

September 9 — Lunar Calendar

DOUBLE NINTH FESTIVAL

Celebrated on the ninth day of the ninth month of the lunar calendar, this festival has lost a lot of its importance in Taiwan. Some people do still follow the traditions, however. According to ancient Chinese thinking, nine is a good, strong number. A double nine might be too strong, though, and this day was thought of as dangerous. The ancient Chinese believed they could overcome this danger by climbing mountains and drinking chrysanthemum wine.

August 8

FATHER'S DAY

Taiwan is the only country in the world to celebrate Father's day on August 8th. In Chinese, the word for eight is "ba," and the date 8/8 sounds very similar to father or "baba." As with Mother's Day, children travel home or call their parents.

October 10

DOUBLE TEN DAY

October 10th marks the start of the Wuchang Uprising in 1911. This mass protest led to the end of imperial rule in China, and the Republic of China was created on January 1st the following year. The day is marked by festivities outside the Presidential Building in Taipei. The celebrations include the raising of the flag and the playing of the national anthem.

Answer Key

CHAPTER 1

Reading Comprehension / p. 13

1 d 2 b 3 d 4 a 5 c

Vocabulary Test / p. 16

1 humid 2 located in 3 landscapes
4 uninhabitable 5 rural 6 ferry
7 cherry blossoms 8 boundary 9 fantastic
10 Saltwater 11 In addition to 12 as a result

CHAPTER 2

Reading Comprehension / p. 21

1 b 2 a 3 c 4 d 5 c

Vocabulary Test / p. 24

1 i 2 a 3 c 4 g 5 k 6 b
7 l 8 f 9 h 10 j 11 d 12 e

CHAPTER 3

Reading Comprehension / p. 29

1 b 2 d 3 a 4 c 5 d

Vocabulary Test / p. 32

1 tribal 2 racial 3 fluent 4 distinct
5 overwhelming 6 categorized 7 descended
8 colonial 9 open-minded 10 comprises

CHAPTER 4

Reading Comprehension / p. 37

1 b 2 a 3 d 4 c 5 a

Vocabulary Test / p. 40

1 worshipped 2 mercy 3 harmony 4 incense
5 bearing 6 regarded 7 predict 8 morality
9 missionaries 10 Buddhism

CHAPTER 5

Reading Comprehension / p. 45

1 a 2 c 3 b 4 b 5 d

Vocabulary Test / p. 48

1 d 2 h 3 j 4 c 5 l 6 l
7 f 8 e 9 k 10 a 11 b 12 g

CHAPTER 6

Reading Comprehension / p. 55

1 c 2 b 3 a 4 b 5 d

Vocabulary Test / p. 58

1 g 2 c 3 k 4 i 5 l 6 d
7 b 8 e 9 f 10 h 11 j 12 a

CHAPTER 7

Reading Comprehension / p. 63

1 a 2 d 3 c 4 d 5 b

Vocabulary Test / p. 66

1 Navigating 2 invented 3 routes 4 privacy
5 extensive 6 scooters 7 terminal 8 license
9 pedaling 10 problematic 11 transit 12 fares

CHAPTER 8

Reading Comprehension / p. 71

1 d 2 a 3 d 4 b 5 c

Vocabulary Test / p. 74

1 facilities 2 accommodation 3 spacious
4 furnished 5 coastal 6 lavish 7 gorgeous
8 extravagantly 9 upmarket 10 vacancies
11 coupon 12 in mind

CHAPTER 9

Reading Comprehension / p. 81

1 d 2 b 3 a 4 b 5 c

Vocabulary Test / p. 84

1 Stir-fired 2 deep-fried 3 spits 4 textures
5 ingredients 6 protein 7 banquet 8 Shellfish
9 consumed 10 intestines 11 cultivation 12 herbs

CHAPTER 10

Reading Comprehension / p. 89

1 a 2 d 3 b 4 c 5 b

Vocabulary Test / p. 92

1 vendors 2 stall 3 skewered 4 gravy 5 stinky
6 scent 7 ferment 8 pickled 9 omelet
10 appearance 11 fillings 12 hollow

CHAPTER 11

Reading Comprehension / p. 97

1 b 2 a 3 d 4 c 5 b

Vocabulary Test / p. 100

1 incorporates 2 originates 3 delicate
4 foundation 5 aromatic 6 intense 7 shallots
8 cured 9 authentic 10 packed 11 contrasting
12 a lot more

CHAPTER 12

Reading Comprehension / p. 105

1 b 2 a 3 c 4 d 5 c

Vocabulary Test / p. 108

1 h 2 e 3 i 4 l 5 k 6 c
7 d 8 f 9 a 10 b 11 g 12 j

CHAPTER 13

Reading Comprehension / p. 113

1 b 2 a 3 c 4 d 5 d

Vocabulary Test / p. 116

1 consisted of 2 essential 3 vermicelli
4 minimal 5 stewed 6 portions 7 combination
8 vinegar 9 oodles 10 chewy

CHAPTER 14

Reading Comprehension / p. 121

1 d 2 a 3 c 4 a 5 b

Vocabulary Test / p. 124

1 d 2 h 3 g 4 l 5 f 6 j
7 c 8 a 9 k 10 i 11 b 12 e

CHAPTER 15

Reading Comprehension / p. 131

1 b 2 a 3 d 4 c 5 b

Vocabulary Test / p. 134

1 rivals 2 agricultural 3 Consumerism
4 gadgets 5 retail 6 dominated 7 majestic
8 luxury 9 pedestrians 10 handicrafts
11 accessories 12 hang out

CHAPTER 16

Reading Comprehension / p. 139

1 c 2 a 3 b 4 b 5 d

Vocabulary Test / p. 142

1 cabinets 2 antlers 3 Funguses 4 aromas
5 produce 6 complex 7 subtle 8 connoisseur
9 carry 10 stationery 11 merchandise
12 toiletries

CHAPTER 17

Reading Comprehension / p. 147

1 b 2 d 3 b 4 a 5 c

Vocabulary Test / p. 150

1 h 2 l 3 f 4 i 5 g 6 a
7 k 8 d 9 c 10 e 11 b 12 j

CHAPTER 18

Reading Comprehension / p. 155

1 c 2 a 3 c 4 b 5 d

Vocabulary Test / p. 158

1 renovate 2 architecture 3 customary
4 specializes 5 surrounding 6 picturesque
7 merchant 8 wares 9 Baroque
10 run-of-the-mill

CHAPTER 19

Reading Comprehension / p. 163

1 d 2 a 3 b 4 c 5 a

Vocabulary Test / p. 166

1 attractions 2 surrounded 3 a big hit 4 cutlery
5 purchase 6 kiddie 7 hoops 8 prefer 9 local
10 entertaining 11 containers 12 reduced

CHAPTER 20

Reading Comprehension / p. 173

1 d 2 c 3 a 4 d 5 b

Vocabulary Test / p. 176

1 c 2 h 3 a 4 l 5 j 6 i
7 e 8 k 9 b 10 f 11 g 12 d

CHAPTER 21

Reading Comprehension / p. 181

1 b 2 c 3 a 4 b 5 d

Vocabulary Test / p. 184

1 enthusiasts 2 military 3 operations
4 reconstructed 5 shrine 6 worthy 7 invaders
8 consulate 9 residential 10 controversial
11 diplomat 12 sacrificed

CHAPTER 22

Reading Comprehension / p. 189

1 d 2 b 3 b 4 c 5 a

Vocabulary Test / p. 192

1 f 2 a 3 k 4 j 5 c 6 d
7 g 8 b 9 h 10 i 11 l 12 e

CHAPTER 23

Reading Comprehension / p. 197

1 b 2 d 3 a 4 d 5 c

Vocabulary Test / p. 200

1 c 2 f 3 e 4 h 5 a 6 d
7 i 8 l 9 g 10 b 11 j 12 k

CHAPTER 24

Reading Comprehension / p. 207

1 c 2 b 3 a 4 d 5 b

Vocabulary Test / p. 210

1 rugged 2 extreme 3 Recreational
4 adrenaline 5 tandem 6 challenging
7 stunning 8 certification 9 parachute
10 snorkeling

CHAPTER 25

Reading Comprehension / p. 217

1 c 2 d 3 a 4 b 5 a

Vocabulary Test / p. 220

1 respectful 2 behavior 3 etiquette 4 social
standing 5 fairly 6 status 7 gap 8 humiliating
9 Gender differences 10 offensive 11 vulgar
12 uncivilized

CHAPTER 26

Reading Comprehension / p. 225

1 c 2 a 3 d 4 a 5 b

Vocabulary Test / p. 228

1 f 2 g 3 k 4 l 5 c 6 j
7 i 8 d 9 h 10 a 11 b 12 e.

CHAPTER 27

Reading Comprehension / p. 233

1 b 2 b 3 a 4 d 5 c

Vocabulary Test / p. 236

1 c 2 g 3 e 4 j 5 a 6 h
7 l 8 i 9 d 10 b 11 f 12 k